The Orphan's Abba

Stories from Orphan Care That Reveal God's Love for You

BY

APRIL JURGENSEN

Cover Design: Marlon Joshua Namoro

Author photo credit: Nickol Teague Photography

To contact the author, write to P.O. Box 47188, Indianapolis, IN, 46247

or email april@apriljurgensen.com

This book is dedicated to my amazing husband, Jim, who not only supports my crazy dreams but also dives in to make them reality. And to our children, Berea and Noah, who have embraced the ride.

What Others Are Saying . . .

The Orphan's Abba is a beautiful and inspiring work containing moving illustrations about orphan care as a reflection of the gospel. April's message rings clear: We are all chosen by God. Her love and passion for orphan care is evident inside every page . . . Her inspiring words ultimately leap from the page and into a reader's heart. After reading *The Orphan's Abba*, you can't help but walk away with a greater sense of God's wonderful love for each of His children.

—Adrian Collins
Writer, Adoption Advocate, Editor for Hope's
Promise Adoption and Pregnancy Blog
Known to made sudden stops for coffee shops and
indie bookstores

April Jurgensen takes us on a journey into some of the roughest orphanages and divulges gut-wrenching stories of children she knows. But she doesn't leave you there. She leads you right back to the Father, and shares what He has revealed to her. With decades of experience in orphan care, April has learned that we, too, are orphans. Her powerful spiritual insights will touch you deeply.

Thank you April, for reminding us of the tender-hearted love of the Father, from your co-workers in the trenches!

Nancy Hathaway
Director, Heart for Orphans

I have worked with orphaned children for the last decade and can testify to the personal transformation April so vividly portrays which results from walking alongside these precious ones. In every story April tells, there's brokenness, injustice and pain, yet in the same narrative, growth, redemption and healing. I felt the weight of her reminder that we're truly all orphaned juxtaposed with the freedom of knowing God loves with abandon and is reckless in His pursuit of each of us revealing more of Himself to us over time, at the right time. Sit deep with this book and bring a box of tissues.

Ann Smith
Missionary in Kenya with Oasis for Orphans
Shameless Coffee ~~Connoisseur~~ Addict
and Closet Bird Nerd

The Orphan's Abba vividly paints a picture of the orphan experience. With authenticity, April Jurgensen gives voice to "the least of these" as the reader ventures into the relationship God seeks with His creation. Each page turn will unveil a quiet crisis and illuminate a faithful Father.

Jennifer Caister
The Boaz Project Board Member
Great Eater of Chocolate Due to Adoptive Parenting

Who are the orphans? We've known the dictionary's basic definition as being "a child without a mother and father." April's book broadened my initial perspective in a profound and new way. I've learned that without

God I myself am a vulnerable orphan. The parallels are insightful and thought provoking.

Ed Schwartz
Loving Shepherd Ministries –
Director of New Initiatives and Founder
Someday hoping to graduate from
Kindergarten class of "Orphan Care 101"

In this book, April shares a deeply personal story of the specific way that God called her to care for some of the most vulnerable children in the world, abandoned by their biological parents and by a system that exhibits the harsh effects of institutional care. Her stories will draw you in and tug at you with the questions of how to respond as you learn more about the deep needs in the world around us. She asks important questions about what it looks like for the Church, the body of believers, to live into God's command "to visit orphans and widows" (James 1:27) and to pray "Thy kingdom come."

Take this book and settle in a quiet space with an open heart. Take part in the journey through hearing stories that may unsettle your soul and possibly cause you to weep. Allow your heart to be open to learning more about the heart of God for each of us, as we too are broken and orphaned but also loved by an almighty God.

Scott Moeschberger, Ph.D.
Professor of Psychology
Director, Initiatives for Vulnerable and
Orphaned Children, Taylor University
Past-President, Division 48 of the American
Psychological Association
Master baker wannabe

I highly recommend *The Orphan's Abba*. April Jurgensen's writing reflects the heart of God and the heart of the orphan as she tells the reader about her journey into orphan care. Her stories are compelling, and her use of Scripture adds powerful spiritual insight.

The Orphan's Abba, though not a technical book on orphan care, serves as a practical and spiritual guide-post for those contemplating this journey and reminds anyone . . . of the love of the Father for the orphan as He sends, guides, provides and sustains in the midst of our service to the children to whom God declares He is their Abba.

Michael Douris
President, Orphan Outreach
Board Member, The Christian Alliance for Orphans
Favorite title: Gramps

Contents

Foreword

I grew up with amazing parents who loved me like crazy, and I had four sweet brothers; the two older ones were overly protective, and the two younger ones gave me more admiration than I deserved. Being raised in a Christian home, I found God early in my life, which anchored me through challenging times. Unfortunately, my idyllic growing up years didn't shield me from pain, and there was one sadness so profound that it changed my view of the world.

After a relationship lasting nearly five decades, a significant person in my life rejected me, and I was powerless to change the situation. I was devastated! As God would have it, it was at the same time that I was researching and writing a book called *The Global Orphan Crisis*. I didn't see the significance at first, but one day when I was trying to understand the plight of being orphaned, I realized that because of my rejection experience, in a very small way, I knew what it felt like to be abandoned, orphaned, and alone.

One young lady I met also had similar feelings. I met Vicky at a children's home in Peru. Vicky was a vibrant, energetic eight-year-old with a beautiful smile. That hadn't always been the case, however. At age three she was found in front of a market with a handwritten sign around her neck that read, "Take me home, I'm to be given away." While it is unclear the circumstances that brought her to that moment, no doubt she was too young to even know the dangerous situation that she was in. Thankfully, a caring person found her and brought her to my friend Doris, who had founded a small children's home in the area. Doris and her team took Vicky in, cared for her, loved her like Jesus loved her, and gave her a new name and a beautiful future.

As earthly companions on this journey we call life, all of us have experienced in a large or small way what it feels like to be rejected, abandoned, and alone. And yet, we also know that God created us uniquely in His image and loves us so much that He sent His only Son to take the place for our sin. And just like Vicky, you are adored by our heavenly Father.

The book you now hold in your hands grew in April's heart through two decades of serving children from difficult places. A wife, mom, ministry leader, friend, and mentor, April's stories of orphaned and vulnerable children will break your heart, open your eyes, encourage your soul, and point you to Jesus!

Diane Lynn Elliot
Writer, photographer, orphan and vulnerable child advocate
Documentary producer wannabe

Introduction

HOW TO READ THIS BOOK

When I was a little girl, I was surrounded by friends who'd been adopted. My parents explained that they weren't born into their families but had been chosen to be in them.

One day, the thought struck me that maybe I was adopted, too. I asked my parents, and though they denied it, I still suspected that maybe they were keeping my true origins a secret.

My mother presented a picture of herself when she was pregnant, but I argued that it could have been from when she was expecting my sister. After lots of scrounging, my mother produced a picture with both her pregnant self and my sister in it.

Little did she know, that photo dashed my hopes. You see, I wanted to be "chosen." I wanted to know that my parents had not just accepted whatever came to them, but that they had made a deliberate choice to select me as their little girl.

Well, God has a funny way of preparing us for His plan. I eventually gained a brother through adoption and married an adoptee. Then God called me into orphan ministry.

For two decades now, I've been blessed to know orphaned children, to see their resilience, to hear their stories, to cheer them on. And God has taught me so much through them—about His character, His love, and His choice to adopt us as His own. These precious children have shed new light on the Scriptures for me. They've challenged my faith and touched my core. God has used them repeatedly to speak to that little girl heart that's still somewhere inside me . . . that deep soul-longing to be chosen for love.

This book is not a clinical approach to orphan care, though we will look at some methods attachment therapists recommend for helping children heal. It's not a case for adoption, though I do sing its praises. It's not a memoir, though I tell a lot of stories.

Rather, these chapters are full of illustrations of how orphan care is a reflection of the gospel message. They will demonstrate how we are like orphaned children in so many ways and how God cares for us better than any human parent ever could. They're intended to open your eyes, encourage your heart, and bolster your faith.

Orphan care is a reflection of the gospel message.

My hope for this book is that it will speak to your heart, assuring you that *you* have been chosen and are loved.

First John 3:1 says, "Behold what manner of love

the Father has bestowed on us, that we should be called children of God!" (NKJV).

I love verses that begin with the word *behold*. It's the King James way of saying "Hold it right there! Stop. Take note. Pay attention. Ponder this!"

My prayer is that this book will help you do just that: ponder what love our Father has given us.

CHAPTER 1

The Call

HOW THE JOURNEY BEGAN

My life was completely altered by a TV show . . . that I never even saw!

It was 1999, and I was a contented Hoosier housewife. My children, ages six months and two years, were my world. I had many of their well-chewed board books memorized, and I carried Cheerios wherever I went.

When I could grab a brief respite in the afternoon while my little ones napped, I would alternate between removing the maple syrup stains from their clothes and scrubbing the mountain of dishes left in the sink.

One day, while my two pint-sized blessings were nestled in for naps, I was vacuuming up graham cracker crumbs when the phone rang.

"April, did you see that thing last night on *20/20* about Russian orphans?" my friend on the other end of the line asked.

I indicated I hadn't, and she continued. She spoke of children banging their heads against their crib rails—children who were too old, really, to be left in cribs—and rocking back and forth. She told of babies dying because they couldn't yet crawl to the bottles that had been tossed onto their mattresses. She spoke of infants lying on soiled bed linens and older children who were drugged to make warehousing them simpler.

Once she grew quiet, I spoke up. "Wow! That's really sad." Then I hung up the phone and went about my day without giving the conversation a second thought.

But then the next day, when my darlings were catching some shut-eye, my phone rang again. I turned off the water at the sink where I was washing bottles to answer.

"April! Did you see that thing a couple nights ago on *20/20* about Russian orphans?" another friend asked.

"No, but Jennifer called me yesterday to tell me about it," I answered.

"Well," this friend launched in, "this mom told her child she was a big girl now and it was time to go to school. She said she was dropping her off at kindergarten and would be back in the afternoon. She left her on the steps of an orphanage instead and never went back!"

"Wow! That's really sad," I responded. Then I hung up the phone and went about my day, still not suspecting my life was about to change.

However, the following day—for the third day in a row—I got another phone call during naptime. "April, did you see that thing the other night . . . I think it was on *60 Minutes* . . ."

"*20/20* about Russian orphans?" I interrupted.

"Yes! You saw it?" came the reply.

"No," I answered, "but this is the *third* phone call I've gotten about it." I hoped that would be enough to deter the caller from elaborating further on such a depressing topic. But it wasn't.

"Oh my goodness!" she exclaimed. "There was this woman who couldn't afford to keep both her son and her daughter. So she had to decide which child she would keep and which she would take to the orphanage."

As the mother of both a son and a daughter, I instantly imagined myself in that woman's position. I didn't really hear the rest of my friend's ramblings for all the noise in my head. *An impossible decision!* I thought.

Finally, when I hung up the phone that day, I wondered, *Lord, is that You calling?* But as quickly as the question crossed my preoccupied mind, I immediately doubted the possibility, thinking, *Nah . . . what's all this got to do with* me?

My Burning Bush

You would think by the third phone call that God would have had my attention, but distracted as I was by my own child-rearing agenda, I explained it all away.

You see, I had lived in Russia for two years and moved back to Indiana just about three years prior to these phone calls. I reasoned that this was why the three callers decided to tell me about the TV show. Apparently it was haunting, and they felt the need to tell *somebody*. My connection to Russia just made me the logical choice. I had yet to acknowledge that God had employed my friends as messengers in disguise . . . until I sensed Him speak to me directly.

In the days that followed, the Lord braided those three phone calls into my memory and began hounding me in earnest. When I spent time reading the New Testament each morning, suddenly verses about the orphaned and the fatherless started jumping out at me. *I've read these books of the Bible before. Why haven't I ever noticed God's passion for the orphan?* I pondered.

At last, I stumbled upon what I refer to as my "burning bush" experience. It was when I came face-to-face with James 1:27: "Religion that God our Father accepts as pure and faultless is this: to look after orphans and widows in their distress and to keep oneself from being polluted by the world."

Wow. There it was in black and white: pure and faultless religion includes caring for the orphan.

Now, I realized that religion is not the same thing as salvation. We are not saved by any works, including caring for the orphan. Scripture makes it clear repeatedly that we are saved by faith in Jesus Christ alone. Religion is the way we live out that faith.

Having accepted Christ as a very young child, I've always wanted my life to glorify Him, to evidence His work in my feeble, frail self. I want my religion—the way I practice my faith—to be acceptable to God. James 1:27 communicated how I could do just that: by looking after widows and orphans in their distress.

In that verse, I saw for the first time that the church—every one of its members—is called to care for orphans. I also felt God was pointing me to something, to a specific role He wanted me to play. Immediately, those three phone calls I had received a couple weeks earlier came to mind. *Lord, what are you trying to tell me? I wondered. What is it you want me to do?*

Just like Moses in his burning bush experience, I had a lot of questions for God, questions rooted in disbelief that He could use me to accomplish a task as daunting as caring for orphans.

What am I supposed to do about these orphans in Russia? I demanded. *I am not a social worker. I have no training or knowledge of the orphanage system in the States or in Russia.*

"*I know their needs. In fact, I know every hair on their heads,*" came the clear, though inaudible, response.

But, I don't know what to do with them. I'm horrible at working with large numbers of children, I argued.

"*I have a lot of children, and I'm pretty good at taking care of them,*" was the rebuttal.

But . . . have you noticed? I live in Indiana now. That's a long way from Russia. How can I do anything from here? Huh? Huh? Clever me. Surely, I had stumped God now!

"*Ah. But I am everywhere,*" He assured me.

Like Moses, I was faced with a simple reality: God wasn't giving me a job. He was giving me the opportunity to watch Him work.

For the first time, thoughts of helpless children distracted my thoughts during the day and often prevented my sleep at night. I was troubled by the stories my friends had shared over the phone, and I held my own two children even more tightly than before.

> *Like Moses, I was faced with a simple reality: God wasn't giving me a job. He was giving me the opportunity to watch Him work.*

As only God could orchestrate, all of these inexplicable incidents happened while I was preparing to return to Russia for a short visit. As I obtained my letter of invitation and began applying for my visa, things only became more bizarre.

Friends and acquaintances started walking up to me, handing me money, and saying, "When you go back to Russia, can you see to it that this gets to an orphanage?"

What? I had told no one but my husband about the way God had been chasing me with thoughts of orphans. And he had told no one.

Now, at this time, my husband, Jim, and I had worked for a mission organization for nearly a decade, but fundraising had never been quite this easy. Normally we had to tell someone we were trying to raise money before they started giving it to us!

I could not ignore that God was up to something . . . even when I tried.

Beginning the Journey

By the time I started packing for the trip, I had too much donated cash to land in Russia and just start handing it out . . . especially at that time, when the Russian exchange rate on the dollar was so high.

So, I went to Walmart. *I'm a mom. I can do this,* I thought. *I know what children need.* So I began filling a cart with Tylenol, socks, and underwear. I bought bibs and toothbrushes, soap and shampoo.

I sat on the suitcases to zip them closed and boarded the plane.

Before we could even get off the ground, I discovered that the family seated in the row in front of me was returning to their work in an orphanage in Moscow. God definitely had my attention.

So about the time the flight attendants were pulling their carts down the aisle to serve hot sandwiches, I leaned forward, "Did you guys by any chance see a thing on *20/20* about orphans in Russia a few weeks ago?" I asked.

Well, not only had they seen the program, but part of it had been filmed in one of the orphanages where they worked!

"That's the problem with Westerners," the husband said as he summed up the program for me. "I mean, I know they mean well and everything, but they send all this aid over to Russia to try to help, but most of it sits outside the orphanage and rots or walks out the backdoor [with staff] and gets sold on the streets, never helping the children at all!"

By now I was completely aghast because, though I was not willing to admit it to this fine gentleman, that's *exactly* what I had intended to do. There, in the belly of that very plane, were two suitcases that I had filled with aid supplies, bought with donated funds, and planned to drop off at an orphanage.

Exasperated, I reached for my tray of food. As I bowed my head to give thanks for it, I leveled with God. *Ugghhh! I am so confused! I am trying hard to figure this all out, trying to be obedient and follow your leading. But you're not making it easy. I'm done here. If you want these suitcases full of stuff to get to orphans and stay there, you're going to have to do it. Amen!*

I believe this is the point when God smiled broadest. *"At last,"* He must have mused, *"she is out of the way."*

As I munched my thick brownie, the high point of my airplane fare, I started thinking, *What's the best way to ensure the treasures stowed below would ever get to—and possibly even stay with—the orphans they were intended to help?*

Think like a Russian, I thought. *I need to find someone who knows someone who works in an orphanage.* After two years living in the culture, I knew the importance of personal connections.

As soon as I arrived, I began asking all my Russian friends, "Do you know anyone who works in an orphanage?" Within two days, I had found connections in two orphanages near the city where I had lived. One was for preschoolers; the other, for babies. I divvied up the items in the suitcases accordingly and headed, fearlessly, to the homes that would rock my world.

My Introduction to Russia's Orphanages

Thankfully, the preschool orphanage was first. I was caught off guard by the cleanliness of the facility and the friendliness of the staff. The director, a matronly woman in her mid-fifties, greeted me with a broad smile accented by deep, pleasant dimples. Her blue eyes sparkled when she accepted the gifts.

"What are the things you need most for the children?" I queried, partly for the information and partly to make conversation. She listed numerous items from the top of her head, a premeditated wish list for sure. School supplies, winter boots, and slippers topped the list.

She allowed me to visit two of the four groups of children in her orphanage. In one, sleepy three-year-olds were rubbing their eyes and stretching as they moved from their naps to bundle up and head outside.

The caretaker pointed at a little girl, "She has not been here long," she informed me. "She was at home with her mother and was very sick with a high fever. She went to climb into bed with her mother, but her mom's 'client' of the evening didn't like a child joining them in the bed. He threw her from their third-story window. Thankfully, she landed in a trash bin or would have certainly died. Someone heard her cries and found her."

I wasn't sure how to respond. I was mortified, but feared showing it in front of the little girl who had just been the audience of her own tragic story. I simply shook my head in disbelief.

After visiting another group of groggy preschoolers, I thanked the director with a handshake and headed to the baby home with Tylenol, bibs, and blankets in hand. I took a deep breath, wondering what I would see.

When we pulled up to the building, I was unimpressed. The gray cinder block building looked much like all the other Soviet structures surrounding it. But for a very small sign by the door, one would never have guessed it housed babies.

When I stepped inside, I was instructed to put "baxhilee" (blue cloth booties) over my shoes. Intended to help keep the floors free of dirt and germs, the poufy footwear over my dress shoes made me feel a bit awkward.

We stepped inside the dimly lit facility. The hallways were clean but stark. No paintings, photos, or murals donned the cream-colored walls.

My interpreter and friend, Svetlana, and I were escorted to the head doctor's office, where we sat through a lengthy dissertation about the conditions of the infants in the orphanage. We were told there were over one hundred babies in the facility, most of whom had living parents who had rejected them for some reason.

Over one hundred infants rejected by their parents, I repeated in my head. It didn't seem possible.

At last, they allowed us to enter a room of babies. The space was occupied by large, brightly colored playpens, each with several babies inside. The toys off to the side of the room looked like they had never been used. Svetlana noticed me looking at them. "From adoptions," she whispered. "The foreign parents are required to donate something to the orphanage when they come for their children."

The babies were adequately dressed, and the room seemed tidy, if not overly sterile. I noted, however, that there was one caretaker for fifteen babies.

Just as I was about to ask if I could pick up a pale-faced, curly-haired girl from her playpen, the doctor whisked us off to another group.

The toddlers I encountered there were adorable but oddly silent. They moved almost in unison, getting up from their naps, putting on their street clothes and shoes, sitting down in their chairs. Each knew where to find his own things and how to put them on independently. No chatter broke the still air; no laughter filled the expanse of their group room.

The doctor pointed to a boy with dark hair and large brown eyes, "This boy will be adopted by a French family," she said proudly.

Next they led me toward another room, but announced that foreigners were not allowed to enter it. Then, without mentioning that they were making an exception for me (or why), the doctor pushed open the aqua door. It wasn't clear whether she was warning me not to follow her or just trying to make me feel special or cautious with her statement. I decided to follow, realizing I could always appear as though I hadn't understood her Russian if she became angry that I entered.

"This is for children who have serious conditions," she explained. "They are unable to learn like the others. They stay here until they are seven years of age."

I glanced around the room. Twelve small cribs were squeezed within its walls. The smell of urine was formidable. The walls were icy white.

I peered into a crib. The child lying within stared vacantly into the air, appearing unaware of my presence. In the crib next to him was a girl who bore the telltale features of Down syndrome. I greeted her in a soft, high voice I usually reserve for infants, though she was likely five.

The doctor called my attention to a rather tall boy whose crib rested against the back wall. "This boy also has Down syndrome," she announced grimly. Then she clucked her tongue a few times, "Though he is seven, he can do nothing but lie here in his crib and drool."

I was outraged! Any child left in a crib for seven years will do nothing but lie there and drool. This boy's parents had abandoned him, and for all practical purposes, the system had, too. I wanted to pull the boy from his crib and hold him close to my heart as I ran from the building and boarded a plane for home.

But having been given entrance to a room where foreigners are prohibited, I bit my lip instead. The best chance for change to the system was for people to learn about its atrocities, and that would never happen if I erupted and prevented others from ever entering this "lying down" room.

I left discouraged, disgusted, and in despair.

After these two orphanage visits, I needed to decide what to do with the more than three hundred dollars that remained of the donated money. Having certainly enjoyed more warm fuzzies at the preschool orphanage than at the infant one, I determined I would head to the central department store and purchase a few things that the director had mentioned.

I began with school supplies: paper, pens, pencils, markers, notebooks, and rulers. I bought everything in bulk. Then I headed to the shoe department and bought all the snow boots and slippers I could locate in sizes appropriate for preschoolers. After that, I bought as many towels as I could find. And with the money left over, I bought toys . . . lots and lots of toys: balls, board games, stuffed animals, and coloring books.

I created quite a scene. In those days, the stores in Russia were relatively well stocked, but no one was buying; the economy had taken such a hit. So my spending created a sort of parade, with employees following me from department to department.

When my shopping spree came to an end, the manager—who had heard by now that I was buying for a local orphanage—offered to let me use the store's van to deliver all my purchases.

With a cargo van filled from front to back and top to bottom, I returned to the preschool orphanage.

The director was summoned before the vehicle had reached the door. She stepped outside into the snow without her coat. When we opened the back door of the van, tears came to her eyes. She reached for my face and kissed my cheeks, alternating sides and repeating, "God bless you."

I was humbled by her blessing. It was she who deserved it. She was caring for children with few resources and doing a good job of it. I had done nothing but spend other people's money. I knew I didn't deserve her gratitude.

My new friend called her assistants to come and unload the van while she took me by the hand to her office, where tea was soon prepared. Warming myself over the cup, I listened to her challenges in caring for the children in her orphanage. Disarmed by the presents I brought, she shared that the government, though responsible for these children, did not provide sufficiently for their needs.

While she was still talking, we were called into a neighboring assembly hall. There, the staff had set up all the toys they had pulled from the van. Then they called in the children.

It Gets Personal

The first boy who walked in caught my eye and took my breath away. He looked just like childhood pictures of my husband! He walked over to a ball and rolled it between his hand and the floor.

I sat, entranced by the familiarity. I wondered if maybe a Kazak heritage had blended with Russian to create a similar appearance to my husband's Chinese and Caucasian fusion.

When I told the director he looked just like my husband, she smiled. "Dima's a good boy," she said. "He does well in school and is kind to the other children."

"Can he be adopted?" I asked.

"No. His mother's rights are protected because she is a quadriplegic," the director responded. "Though no one from his family has ever come to visit, sent a letter, or called him, he cannot be adopted. I even went to his mother's home and tried to persuade her to do what is right by him. But she asked me, 'If I let him go, who will take care of me in my old age?'"

I wondered, *But who will take care of him now? And what will motivate him to care for his mother later?*

"It is a sad situation," she continued, "since he has just turned seven and will soon move to another orphanage where things are more difficult. And it will be impossible to find a family as he ages."

I didn't understand how foreboding her words were until I later visited a school-aged orphanage.

Group by group, the children came, looking at the toys and revealing discolored baby teeth as they grinned from excitement. They bounced the balls and tried the plastic bowling set. Girls cradled dolls and boys made car noises as they drove vehicles around the brown and cream rug. I wished those who had handed me money could see the joy they created.

I left the orphanage that day pondering what would become of Dima.

I had done my duty. I had seen to it that the money people had given me had been used for things for an orphanage, and I believed most of the things would stay there. At last, I would have God off my back.

It was time to go home, and I tried to turn my thoughts there.

Yet, as I rode in the taxi back toward Moscow, a sinking feeling returned to my gut. I realized that I had just put a tiny Band-Aid on a huge, gaping wound. What these children needed was Jesus—and I had given them socks and underwear!

Unable to push the children I had met out of my stream of consciousness, I acknowledged their stories were no longer tidbits on news magazines. They were stories of real children—with names and talents and wounds. Their cries were now audible. Their haunting eyes chilled me. All I had heard about on *20/20* I had now seen firsthand.

I knew I had to do something . . . and that I could not do it alone.

As I spent the night in Moscow before an early morning flight home, I wrestled with God. He had opened my eyes to the plight of the Russian orphan, but I still didn't know why. What else was I to do?

By the wee morning hours, I had settled on a plan.

When daylight came and my friends arrived to take me to the airport, I asked one of them if—just in case people back home would be interested in helping orphans—I could hire him to administrate the operation. If I sent him money, would he go to the orphanage director and ask what they needed most? Then, would he go and buy those things, never handing out cash?

I had written out a contract he could give the orphanage director, requiring her to allow him to enter the orphanage at any time to see how the donated items were being used. If the donations weren't there or weren't being used for the children, we wouldn't work there anymore. Game over.

He agreed to help.

Of course, neither of us dreamed what God would do through the arrangement.

Within days of my return home, I found myself telling everyone I saw about the children I had met, especially Dima. I wrote an email to friends from out of town and talked to my church's missions committee.

I was finally sensing that God had something greater than two suitcases in mind . . . and that I owed a debt of gratitude to *20/20*. But I still didn't realize that what had begun out of a sheer desire to obey God's command in James 1:27 would change the course of my life. I didn't discern that orphans would rock my theology. I hadn't expected that these children would pierce my heart. I never imagined that the little faces I had yet to meet would nimbly change my perspective on everything.

All I knew was that God had turned three phone calls into a calling. And now, I could not hang up and walk away.

Questions to Ponder or Discuss

Before reading chapter one, read James 1:27 and record or share your thoughts.

After reading the chapter:

1) How do you respond when you see TV shows like the one described in this chapter?

2) Have you ever had a "burning bush" experience, where God communicated His leading in your life in a way that felt individual to you and quite obvious? How did you respond?

3) Have you ever had your theology "rocked"? If so, how?

CHAPTER 2

Command

HOW OBEDIENCE YIELDS CHANGE

Even as my vehicle pulled up to the facility, I could sense this experience was going to be different. The aging structure sagged wearily and almost boasted of its distinct odor. I braced myself for what I might see.

Several months had passed since my first foray into Russia's orphanage system. I'd found some support for a ministry to orphans and formed The Boaz Project as an official non-profit organization, and we were now offering monthly support and weekly Bible classes to orphans. I returned to the former Soviet country, scrambling to learn all I could. I was about to enter a school-aged children's orphanage for the first time.

Once inside, I was escorted by a stiff guard to the director's office. Sternly, the director glanced at me above her reading glasses but didn't speak.

"Hello," I said timidly. For some reason, I had greeted her in English, and though I had an interpreter (my friend, Svetlana) in tow, I didn't feel the need for her to interpret.

The woman glanced at Svetlana, as if to indicate that she should have prevented this foreigner from distracting her from the papers on her desk. Then she sighed.

"May I speak with you for just a moment?" I asked sheepishly.

Without waiting for interpretation, the director waved her hand, motioning for us to sit down at the table before her—a gesture that was both an invitation to enter and a brush off. I had barely begun explaining that I came bearing gifts from friends in America when another suited woman peeked around the corner and interrupted me. I understood that someone was here and coming to the office, but I did not catch who.

With another sigh, the director took off her glasses and nodded that entry was granted.

Two children, identical in appearance, turned the corner. I could not determine their gender but guessed them to be around seven years of age. They wore coats that looked warm but worn.

"Your names?" demanded the director. The children stared, frozen in fear.

"Your names!" she repeated more loudly. The children blinked but did not even cast glances at one another.

"You must give me your names!" the director yelled as she rose from her desk.

One poor child swallowed hard before replying, "Ola."

Girls, I deduced. I wondered if they had come from a home or another orphanage. I imagined how they must be feeling either way. I blinked back the tears welling in my eyes.

"Ah, Ola, and . . ." the militant director waited for the second child to answer, but, gripped by fear, the girl remained silent.

As Ola opened her mouth to answer for her twin, she was cut off. "Your sister must learn to speak for herself. Does she not understand Russian? I have asked for your names. It is a simple question. If you don't learn to speak for yourselves, you will not survive here. Now, young lady, I am asking for the last time. What is your name?"

The stunned child remained stoic as a tear trickled down her right cheek. "Nastya," she answered at last.

I realized the director, not knowing I had lived in Russia for two years, had likely assumed I didn't understand the conversation. But even if I hadn't, her tone would have exposed her.

A few more details were discussed, and the stout director waved her arms and raised her voice. I sat stunned, scheming how I could possibly escape and take the frightened girls with me. Yet the brutal reality of the situation broke through my imaginings. The twins were there to stay.

I doubted any of the school supplies or toiletries I carried into that office would go to the children who lived under this woman's "care," but, having announced them as the reason for my visit, I was forced to leave them. And after just a few minutes of discussion with the director, I did so, reluctantly.

Throughout those early years, encounters like this one became commonplace as I navigated the hidden world of Russia's orphans. Mistreatment was routine; abuse, familiar.

In one orphanage in Russia's Far East, I saw teenage boys beaten and stripped naked for a week because they had run away. I noticed children locked in isolation, fed through a tiny barred window. I found evidence of girls as young as eleven being preyed upon from within and outside the orphanage.

In another, I heard a director referring to the children in her institution as "society's refuse." This was her defense for their maltreatment. Justification for her cruelty.

These barbarities were the things that happened in my presence. I shuddered to think of the horrors that took place in my absence.

The system had effectively gagged those who uncovered the truth. Speak up, and risk being denied entrance to the orphanages—perhaps to the country.

Confident that authorities would look the other way if confronted, I decided to stay silent so I could continue to visit the children . . . and even bring others with me. Our access was a means to bring the children the Good News and hope. If we were kicked out, who would share the hope of Christ with them? Who would tell them they are precious, unique, beautiful, and loved?

Who would tell them about their heavenly Father who adores them . . . so much so that He knows the number of hairs on their heads?

So I restrained myself from whistle-blowing and recruited Russian friends to visit the orphanages. I wrote Bible Discovery curriculum, and I prayed for the children I met.

Simultaneously, I felt powerless against the formidable governing system.

Inside, a spiritual war began to rage. The duplicity stifled me. I started to tussle with God. Doesn't the Bible say He is the orphans' defender? Then where was He? Why wasn't God stopping these atrocities? And why had He awakened me to them, powerless as I am?

A Command . . . And More

In an effort to answer my own questions and doubts, I mentally went back to my "burning bush" experience . . . to the verse that convinced me that God was telling me to care for orphans: "Pure and undefiled religion in the sight of our God and Father is this: to visit orphans and widows in their distress, and to keep oneself unstained by the world" (James 1:27 NASB).

Much like a mother asking her son to clean his room, God needs little justification for asking us to care for orphans beyond, "Because I said so." After all, He is God, and we are not. Yet I sensed God's reasoning was deeper than that, and I longed to understand more.

I must admit: When I first contemplated James 1:27, it struck me as a little odd. Why, given the desperate needs orphans endure, would God ask us to visit them? Why does He not ask us to evangelize them? Certainly it would be helpful for us to feed them! How about clothe them? Then, if those needs are met, certainly it would be helpful to educate them. But visit? It felt superfluous to me.

Why, given the desperate needs orphans endure, would God ask us to visit them?

23

Until I visited them.

By taking God at His word and obeying Him, I gained great insight into His desire for us to simply visit orphans. I saw that God, in His wisdom, proposed a method of changing both orphans and those of us visiting them.

> *God, in His wisdom, proposed a method of changing both orphans and those of us visiting them.*

First, I noticed the impact that the visits had on the children.

Take, for example, a nine-year-old girl I met in one of the Russian orphanages. We'll call her Masha. She was present every day during our VBS, but not one team member managed to make eye contact with her throughout the week. Her quiet voice only spoke up when someone implored her. Otherwise, she sat silently, wringing her hands or scratching her forearms. We could only imagine what Masha had been—or was still going—through.

Oh, she needed food and clothes. She needed to know Jesus loves her. Most of all, she needed to understand that she was safe to experience love—including the love of the one eternal Creator God. She needed someone to be with her.

Or consider Nikita. I met him just a few days after he came to an orphanage in a small city on the European side of Russia. Until the previous week, he had lived with two loving parents not far from the orphanage.

But one night, a fire set their apartment ablaze. Nikita and his dad fled through a window that led to fire escape stairs. His father instructed him to go down the stairs, cross the street, and wait. Then he climbed back into the apartment in hopes of rescuing his wife.

Both parents died in the fire while Nikita watched the flames swallow the apartment whole from across the street.

And so Nikita sat, staring blankly through most of the Vacation Bible School we held in his orphanage that week. He didn't need the games or crafts or even the snacks. He needed someone present, assuring him that he was safe now.

Over the years, I've met these children and thousands more. As we visit them, I've watched eyes brighten and hearts soften. I've witnessed the aloof become engaged and the broken venture a smile . . . not because of some donation we made or elaborate game we played. It was because we gave them dignity by visiting them.

We acknowledged they were human beings by looking in their eyes. We made comical attempts at speaking their language and encouraged their artistic or athletic abilities. We ate side by side with them and learned their names.

It is powerful, this gift of presence.

God's Work in Us

While visiting orphans, we give God the opportunity to work in us, too.

You see, once we have visited orphans, feeding them, clothing them, and even educating them become our priorities. We eagerly seek to bless these children who are precious in God's sight, not

> *While visiting orphans, we give God the opportunity to work in us, too.*

only out of obligation as a believer but also because they have impacted us. They have shuffled our hearts' desires.

It often begins with learning a name, then playing a game. We see the hint of a smile or the swelling of a tear and we are endeared. We learn their stories and are moved—not by the global orphan crisis but by this child we've come to know. This Olya or Igor or Natasha who stands before us.

And at some point along the way, we realize we're not so different from these orphaned children, really. Apart from Christ, we are orphans, not yet reconciled to our Father . . . and we resemble orphans in many ways. Here are just a few:

1) We live under the strain of a misdiagnosis.

I was outraged when I first read that an estimated 80 percent of the children in Russia's orphanages deemed "oligophrenic" ("small-brained" or imbecile) had been misdiagnosed.[1] How could they be wrong about so many children?

I was also furious because I knew the power of such a diagnosis . . . and how it would magnify the stigma of being an orphan in Russian culture.

When a child becomes an orphan in Russia, that status is indicated in his passport and remains there the rest of his life. The damage is significant because Russians use passports in much the same way we use our

---

[1] Human Rights Watch, *Abandoned to the State: Cruelty and Neglect in Russian Orphanages* (New York: Human Rights Watch, 1999).

driver's licenses. Applying for a job? Provide your passport for ID. Registering for classes? Show your passport. Handling a transaction at a bank? You need a passport for that, too.

Once you understand the hardships of being an orphan in Russian society, you realize just how difficult that label can make daily life. Should an orphan survive to age fifty, she will still be prejudged because of a classification that described her many years ago.

Add to all of this a mental, behavioral, or physical impairment? Employment, education, and even relationships are often out of reach.

Suffer all of that when the diagnosis isn't even accurate? Unimaginable!

One day, a psychologist who works in a Russian preschool orphanage showed me one of the activities she uses to test three-year-olds for mental impairment, and the reason for the high rate of misdiagnoses became apparent.

In her office, she proudly pointed to two sandboxes. One contained wet sand. The other, dry. She explained that when the children are invited to play, she notes whether they choose the wet or dry sand. If they choose the wet and build elaborate structures, she said it is clear that those children have many psychological issues they will never be able to overcome.

That "play session" could change the course of a life. The architect of an elaborate sand castle could easily be diagnosed as "uneducable" and set on a trajectory of lifelong institutionalization in mental facilities.

As she spoke, I moved to position myself between her and my three-year-old son. I didn't want him to help himself to the sandboxes. After all, what I had always encouraged as creativity was apparently viewed as an irreversible mental illness!

Over my years working in orphanages, I have seen many evidences of misdiagnoses: physical, behavioral, and mental. Once issued, these labels are permanent and carry full authority.

I've also come to realize that many of us, apart from the light of God's Word, have believed Satan's lies about ourselves. His intentional misdiagnoses hold as much power as if they, too, have the potential to permanently influence our lives. He has convinced us that we are too dumb, too fat, too complicated. He's persuaded us to believe that we could never amount to anything or that we need to clean up before coming to God.

> *Many of us, apart from the light of God's Word, have believed Satan's lies about ourselves.*

Satan has told us we are of no value, and we've believed it.

That misdiagnosis is powerful, friend. It can affect our employment, our education, and even our relationships.

If believed, Satan's lies can set us on a trajectory of imprisonment. The facilities are invisible, but no less formidable or confining than those made of brick and mortar.

2) We're in need of a defender.

One day, while visiting some abandoned infants, I met a baby named Katya. Though she was still young enough to have only mustered some fuzz for hair, Katya had the most alarmingly blue eyes. I'm certain they would have been the first thing I'd noticed about her if it hadn't been for the burn tissue.

The right half of Katya's face and body were covered with scars. Unable to imagine the cause, I asked the woman who was on shift as a caregiver.

She matter-of-factly explained that Katya's mother had left her, and so, by default, Katya's grandmother assumed guardianship. One day, Katya cried and cried. The grandmother grew weary of it and poured boiling water on her to get her to stop.

Katya was rendered a ward of the state. I doubted she would get the skin graft surgeries she so desperately needed to allow for growth. Was she receiving anything for the pain that racked her body day and night? Would someone else take advantage or inflict suffering upon her? How detestable that a grandmother, the one trusted to be Katya's caregiver and defender, had caused such enduring pain!

Again, we are not so unlike the orphans I've met, including Katya. Until we surrender to Christ's lordship over our lives, we are choosing to live independently from God, our defender.

Of course, Katya had no say in what happened to her. Given the choice, surely she would have wanted someone to protect her. Yet, if that seems obvious, why is it that human nature chooses otherwise when it comes to God? We've all at some point proudly resisted God's ways. Isaiah 53:6 puts it this way: "We all, like sheep, have gone astray, each of us has turned to our own way."

When we strike out on our own, outside of God's will and commands, we choose to reject Him as our defender. We invite chaos and consequences. We function as wards of the state, uncertain that our needs will be met, susceptible to suffering.

We've all at some point proudly resisted God's ways.

3) We're inept at self-sufficiency.

Artyom and his mother lived in a small village on the edge of a forest. When his mother died (for reasons unknown), Artyom fled from their small house and into the forest, where he lived for months on his own. Frightened, he avoided the edge of the forest that bordered the community he had lived in.

No one knows how Artyom survived; what he ate, where he rested, or how he endured the harsh Russian winter.

When he was found, he wouldn't speak or smile. He was brought to an orphanage where he was called "the wild boy."

Orphanage life, which entails communal living, did not suit Artyom. He refused to eat when the other children ate, to go to the bathroom in synchronization with the others, to nap at the same time as everyone else, or to restrict his play to the assigned area of the orphanage grounds.

Life on his own had hardened Artyom. It made him incapable of living in a group setting, of giving and receiving support or love. He had negotiated terms with hunger. He had stood guard at night. He had known the threat of frost without a covering for his protection.

Friend, we can learn much from Artyom.

When we are tempted to live in isolation, build walls between family members, stay home from church, or erect fences between yards, remember Artyom. Choose to live in community, giving and receiving support and love, because in isolation, you must become familiar with a deep hunger of the heart. You must stand guard, watching for prey without respite from anyone. You must know the cold, wintry seasons of life without the protective covering community can offer.

In isolation, you must become familiar with a deep hunger of the heart.

4) We can be guilty of indiscriminate affection.

So often when we first enter a Russian preschool orphanage, children will come to hang their arms around our waists and call out, "Mama!" or "Papa!" Many newcomers to the orphanage can be flattered, thinking a child has really chosen him and bonded with him. Some children are even adopted because of this emotional experience.

That seems like a good thing until they bring their child home, only to have her run up to a woman in the grocery store, wrap her arms around them, and cry out, "Mama!"

Children who've not attached to a safe and loving adult often attempt attachment with anyone, anywhere. Though their safety is at risk, they're too impulsive to notice. They just need their longing for love satisfied.

Again, we are not so different. If—for any reason—we've chosen not to bond with our heavenly Father, we can desperately search for attachment with anyone, anywhere. Though our safety is at risk, we're too impulsive to notice. We just need our longing for love satisfied.

5) We long to belong.

As I was leaving an orphanage one day, some of the older kids were outside, just hanging out. Tolya, a boy of about thirteen, approached me and said something in rapid Russian. I explained that I didn't understand him and asked him to repeat himself. Again, he spoke so quickly that I couldn't comprehend. I realized he was likely speaking softly and hurriedly so that the others nearby wouldn't hear. So I leaned way in and quietly asked him to say it again, more slowly.

At last, I understood his words: "I want to be adopted!"

It was difficult to leave the orphanage without Tolya that day. He had bravely uttered the inner yearning so many orphans deny—not just openly but internally as well. He had spoken a deep longing that is common to man. He acknowledged that he wanted a family to call him their own.

Though we are born into different circumstances—socioeconomic strata, race, religious environments, and family dynamics—we are all born with this need to belong. Some seek it in healthy ways. Some, not so healthy.

But when we come to understand that we belong in God's family, we can become utterly content. We are safe to admit our needs and grateful that God calls us His own.

Misdirected Angst

As I worked out James 1:27 and visited orphans, I understood that I had been asking the wrong question. I had been asking, "Where is God while orphans suffer?" when I should have been asking, "Where are God's people, who have been called to care for orphans?"

God *has* a plan to care for orphans, and it involves you and me.

It turns out, James 1:27 isn't the only Scripture reference that says so.

> *God* has *a plan to care for orphans, and it involves you and me.*

Isaiah 1:17 contains another command to care for the orphan: "Learn to do right; seek justice. Defend the oppressed. Take up the cause of the fatherless, plead the case of the widow."

In fact, Scripture is full of God's instructions to care for the orphan, as well as the widow, the poor, and the oppressed. So why are these individuals still suffering?

What would it look like if we—all of us who are called by Christ's name—were to take Him seriously in this? What if we all cared for an orphan? What if we adopted, or supported those who do? What if we visited orphans? What if we gave generously? What if we took up their cause?

I imagine it would be a different world, one where orphans would not fret over their next meals or go without medical care. It would be a place where children would be able to trust that they were lovable and that they were loved. In this world where the church is obedient, the fatherless would be introduced to their heavenly Father.

> *My frustrations and anger were misdirected. God had not left these children. We, His church, had.*

If that's true, my frustrations and anger were misdirected. God had not left these children. We, His church, had.

I had.

All too often, I'm wrapped up in building my own little kingdom without giving God permission to distract me with His. But Jesus instructed us to pray, "Thy kingdom come" (Matthew 6:10 KJV).

Thine. Not mine.

God's Coming Kingdom

Scripture describes God's kingdom as a beautiful time and place where there are no orphans, no widows, no tears, and where there is no loneliness. There's no death, sorrow, illness, or pain.

When I write those truths, I can eagerly say, "Thy kingdom come!" And when I think of my orphan friends, I am reminded of the tears they shed in prayer. They long so desperately for a kingdom without death, pain, separation, and ridicule—a world without neglect or abuse, loneliness or hunger.

What is our part in bringing about God's kingdom?

We actually don't have to wonder. He already told us. Micah 6:8 tells us, "What does the LORD require of you? To act justly and to love mercy and to walk humbly with your God."

I've seen glimpses of this kind of kingdom. It isn't

widespread and hasn't gone viral across any culture. It doesn't saturate any society I have visited.

Rather, it's a tiny, joyful subculture. It's a secret society that some modern-day saints recruit for boldly as they live in ways that defy cultural norms and societal expectations. It's a revolution of sorts against the mores of their communities and the traditions of their peoples.

It's a community marked by obedience.

It's people—regular salt-of-the-earth kinds of folks—who actually take God at His Word and share His heart for orphans. It's families who decide it's better to spread the peanut butter (or the lentils or ugali or borscht or bulgogi) a little thinner than to leave a child to the streets.

It's churches who decide that taking care of orphans is a group effort, so they all pitch in to serve foster and adoptive families.

It's good ole souls who nurture and shelter and educate. They wipe runny noses and change soiled sheets. They help practice multiplication tables and advise how to handle bullies. They are parents not by nature but by choice.

It is a microcosm of the kingdom of God on earth. It's a foreshadowing of the heavenly and a foretaste of a new and promised era.

And it begins when we visit orphans.

Questions to Ponder or Discuss

Before reading chapter two, read Isaiah 1:17 and brainstorm ways to apply it.

After reading the chapter:

1) Have you ever had an experience where God's commands made more sense *after* you obeyed (or disobeyed) them? What did you learn from that experience?

2) When have you wanted to state your opinion but felt it wise to remain silent? How did it feel?

3) Have you had the opportunity to visit orphans? What sticks out to you from that experience?

4) What misdiagnosis have you accepted as true about yourself?

CHAPTER 3

Character

HOW ORPHANS TEACH YOU ABOUT GOD'S CHARACTER

As I prepared for our second VBS in a Russian orphanage, selecting a curriculum was a bigger challenge than I expected. I knew it would have to work cross-culturally, avoiding the references many of our themed curricula in the States have to things like newspaper carriers or cowboys. Even "Under the Sea" or "Mountain Explorer" motifs are likely to bewilder children who've never put a toe in the sea or gasped at the sight of mountains.

Yet when I began looking at options, I was astonished to realize the number of references to parents and siblings in most lesson plans. The examples for sharing included brothers and toys. The need for obedience was (understandably) explained in relation to parents. How could orphans relate to those illustrations?

So, having attended numerous Vacation Bible School programs as a child, I resolved to write the curriculum myself. I was very familiar with Daniel and the lion's den, Jonah and the whale, Moses in a basket, and the parting of the Red Sea. It couldn't be too difficult to retell these stories and come up with simple crafts and games to go along with them. I thought that should be easy enough.

Until we actually went to Russia and began the Vacation Bible School.

I believe it was our second day of VBS. I don't remember the particular story we told that day, but the theme was forgiveness. That evening, the team gathered to debrief, as we always do. I asked, "How did today go?"

A college-aged young woman began, "Well, after telling the story, I asked the question about whether they'd ever had to forgive someone. This tiny four-year-old girl raised her hand. When I called on her, she said, 'My mother put me in the oven.'"

We sat in silence.

We had come to teach the Bible, to model Christ's character. I had written a lesson about forgiveness. The truth was, I knew nothing about it compared to this willowy preschooler.

The woman who was supposed to be her nurturer had nearly killed her.

Over the years, this theme has been a constant. The children God has called me to love and serve have faced trials and questions and obstacles I can't imagine.

They have seen the depths of the depravity of man. They have suffered abuse of

> *The children God has called me to love and serve have faced trials and questions and obstacles I can't imagine.*

all forms. They are referred to as "society's refuse," even as others victimize them.

It wasn't too many years later that we were in another orphanage just about twenty miles from that one. We were enjoying a cup of tea with the teenage boys and discussing life's great mysteries.

The topic, once again, turned to forgiveness.

The group became quiet and looked back and forth between two brothers, as if watching a tennis match with no ball.

When I inquired as to what was going on, the younger spoke, "I'm angry with my brother and refuse to forgive him. He has done horrible, horrible things to me. He hasn't acted like a brother, and I won't treat him like one."

Unaware of what this older brother had done, I tried to empathize with the younger, but help him see that a lack of forgiveness would only give bitterness a root in his heart.

He responded, "What I really want to know is—where is God when stuff like that happens?"

I set my cup in its saucer and said a quick and desperate prayer. "He is with you, and He is weeping," I replied.

It is hard for me to tell these children that they need to forgive—not because I'm unconvinced that it's what's best for them, but because I feel unqualified to do so. Who am I to tell orphans who've endured so much loss and pain how to handle it?

Their experiences make my life look like an extended stay at Disneyland.

Their grief forces me to realize I have very little reason to hold any grudge. If they are called to forgive those who've sinned against them, how much more so am I?

When Christ modeled prayer for us, He uttered some challenging words. He asked God to, "forgive us our debts, as we forgive our debtors" (Matthew 6:12).

Sometimes, I wrestle to forgive and find myself having to lay certain hurts before the Lord and release them repeatedly. How much more difficult it must be for some of the orphans I know to forgive the things which have been done to them!

I think that's exactly Christ's point in this prayer, because what God has forgiven is greater still.

My pride, my selfishness, my every sin cannot be made light because they nailed God's one and only perfect Son to a cross. My lack of obedience hurled insults at the Messiah, and my rebellion placed a crown of thorns on His head. As I bruise the Son God sent to save me, He is there, and He is weeping.

My pride, my selfishness, my every sin cannot be made light because they nailed God's one and only perfect Son to a cross.

Yet, He forgives. How can I not forgive those who've wounded me?

If my goal is to be like Christ, then I must allow Him to develop His character in me. Contrary to my wishes, this rarely happens in the midst of sunset walks or shopping sprees. Naiveté is a blissful place, but it teaches me nothing of my need for grace.

Working with orphans, hearing their stories and learning to view the world through their eyes has forced me to examine God's characteristics—like forgiveness—in deeper and more complex ways than I ever would if I were left to interpret everything based on my own experiences.

Naiveté is a blissful place, but it teaches me nothing of my need for grace.

We can intellectually assent that God is forgiving, generous, patient, compassionate, and merciful, a Father to the fatherless. But knowing orphans has helped me gain more intimate knowledge, more depth of insight, into what those words even mean.

More Than a Superhero

Sometimes, seeking to be like God can feel outlandish. I can't imagine having His character or abilities. It's like the childhood question, "If you could have any super power, which would you choose?"

God is all-powerful, which is much better than having to choose just one strength or ability.

He is all-knowing, and there have definitely been days when I've wished I were (and days when I've been glad I'm not).

God is all-seeing, and that sounds pretty cool . . . most of the time.

While we can't be omniscient or omnipresent or omnipotent, we CAN grow in God's character. Just as that tiny preschooler taught me about forgiveness, other children have taught rich lessons of Christlikeness. They have challenged my thinking, humbled my spirit, and matured my faith more than any theologian has. Following are a few of the ways I've been schooled by orphans.

Generosity

> The wicked borrow and do not repay, but the
> righteous give generously.
>
> PSALM 37:21

From the time my children were three and five, they accompanied me and my husband whenever we both traveled overseas. I refused to abandon my children and make them feel like orphans because we were caring for others.

It was on one of his earliest trips that my son Noah developed a friendship with a boy named Zhenya.

Zhenya was a few years older than Noah, but his stature wasn't much greater. His hair was redder than strawberry blond, but not quite as bold as you'd imagine if I just said it was "red." His blue eyes were bright, and his countenance didn't reflect the sorrow of his situation.

Trip after trip, the boys would greet one another with a hug. Without shared language, they played for days and seemed to communicate more fluidly than many of us who share a common language.

Once, as we were leaving the orphanage for the day, I noticed something in Noah's pocket. When I asked him about it, he pulled out a green plastic army man. "Zhenya gave it to me," he said with a smile.

I didn't even know what to say.

I took Noah by the hand and walked with him into the room where Zhenya and six other boys slept. I asked Zhenya if he was certain he wanted to give Noah the army man.

"Yes!" Zhenya answered, "He's my friend."

I could hardly handle his sweetness.

I knew that Zhenya could not have even imagined the mountain of toys that awaited Noah at home. He had tubs of LEGOs and Playmobile sets. He had every Buzz Lightyear a boy could want. He had a Spiderman costume and even carpet skates. He didn't need a green army man.

So I asked Zhenya to show me his things.

He walked to a bedside nightstand and opened the drawer—the one drawer which contained all of his belongings. Inside, he had one book, one picture of some other foreign visitors, a tiny bouncy ball, and a torn filmy parachute I decided must have at one time been attached to the prized army man.

I explained to Noah that those were the only things Zhenya owned.

The boys decided that Noah should keep the Army man. It was a gesture of friendship that bordered on brotherhood. Once offered, it could not be retracted. It had been given selflessly, and—to my surprise—had been received respectfully.

Though not yet school-aged, Noah grasped the magnitude of that seemingly simple gift. Though he had numerous gadgets and gizmos, he treasured the green Soviet Army man.

As of this writing, my son is twenty. Buzz Lightyear made his way to Goodwill. Noah outgrew the Spiderman costume (and, thankfully, the desire to wear it) long ago. The LEGOs are in storage, awaiting the arrival of my grandkids, and the Playmobile sets have been shared with relatives. But the last I knew, that green army man still resided in Noah's closet, a reminder of a friend who taught him what real generosity looks like.

Patience

> Be joyful in hope, patient in affliction, faithful in prayer.
>
> ROMANS 12:12

Often, we've gathered a team after their first day of ministry in Russia's orphanages to debrief and been told, "One of the kids in my group is going home tomorrow!"

In the early days, I got so thrilled by the news. A little one was leaving institutional life to be rejoined to a parent! I would celebrate the prospect with applause and enthusiasm.

But too many times, the team member would return the next evening, only to report that the reunion had been delayed a day. "Her mother will come tomorrow," he'd say.

Day after day, the team member and child would watch and wait with nervous anticipation for the arrival of a parent. Yet the next day would be a repeat of the former. No mother or father came. Hope would be deferred another day. And another. And another. However, the child would never grow weary, lose hope, doubt that Mom would come. She would remain patient in her waiting and hoping.

You see, the team member hadn't gotten his information from a credible orphanage administrator who had official documentation returning guardianship to a parent. Rather, he'd been told by an ever-hopeful child that "Mom's coming to get me. She'll be here soon!"

These days, when a team member announces that a child's parents are coming to take him home, I cringe a bit inside. I hope the intel is accurate, but I fear it's a child's imaginings.

At once, I pity and admire the child. I hurt for the young one who may be disappointed day after day, but I marvel at the patience on display.

The thing is, we have it on credible authority—that of God Himself—that Christ is coming back for us. It is not a false hope, but a promised reality. He has gone to prepare a place for us and one day will usher us there. We are told to watch and wait and minister in His name until that day comes.

I don't know about you, but too often I grow weary of the wait. I lose sight of Christ's imminent return and neglect fervent watchfulness. I forego ministering in His name to seek a little ease and comfort. I get distracted by the trappings of this world and forget to gaze upon the eternal.

Oh, to have the faith—and patience—of a child awaiting his Father's return!

Oh, to have the faith—and patience—of a child awaiting his Father's return!

Compassion

> But you, Lord, are a compassionate and gra-
> cious God, slow to anger, abounding in love and
> faithfulness.
>
> PSALM 86:15

After nearly a decade of working in Russia's orphanages,
we sensed God leading us to broaden our scope and
minister to orphans in other nations. In 2009, He led
us to India.

The first children's home we visited in Bangalore stood
in stark contrast to the state-run institutions we had
become so familiar with in Russia. It was a home, really,
with parents who had obeyed God's leading to care for
orphans.

We were barely inside when the children approached
to greet us, shaking our hands and declaring, "Praise the
Lord!" in turn.

In brightly-colored clothing, the children introduced
themselves. Then they danced and sang for us. They recited
Bible verses and shared their humble meal.

We'd been in the home for several joy-filled hours
when I noticed burn scars on Jennifer's arm. While playing
a game, Jennifer raised her hands, and her sleeve fell to
her shoulder, revealing evidence of trauma her countenance didn't show.

When I asked the house mother about the scars I'd
spotted, she nodded sorrowfully. Then she explained that
Jennifer's father had died. At the funeral, her mother
committed suicide by throwing herself on the funeral pyre.

I didn't know at the time that this used to be a relatively common Hindu practice, as widows feared the shunning and blame associated with a husband's death.

Jennifer may have been unfamiliar with the practice, as well. But when she saw her mother burning, she ran to her and threw herself on her, hoping to rescue her from the flames. Onlookers wrestled to pull Jennifer from her mother. Her life was spared, but her mother's was not.

Bible scholars tell us that the meaning of the word *compassion* is to "suffer with." I can think of no clearer example of suffering with someone than Jennifer's choice to throw herself upon her mother's burning body. To this day, she carries on her flesh the constant reminder of her mother, and the suffering continues.

Once again, an orphan embodies Christ's character for me so poignantly, this time by loving deeply enough to enter another's fire and bear another's pain. This is compassion in its truest from.

Mercy

"Be merciful, just as your Father is merciful."
LUKE 6:36

I couldn't believe God had miraculously reunited us!

Olya and I had spent many hours together when she was growing up in the orphanage. From my first time in that institution, she stayed right by me, as if attached at the hip. And every time I returned, it was the same routine: If I went outside to check on the groups there, she came with me. If I were inside, helping a group with a craft, she made one and gave it to me.

Each year, I would return, and Olya would be a little taller and little more mature. But still she stayed by my side, savoring each moment of individual attention.

It broke my heart, but I wasn't able to visit her region of Russia the year Olya graduated from the orphanage system, and I assumed I'd never see her again.

As state-run institutions, the orphanages are not permitted to give us any forwarding information on the children who leave. So I had no way to find her in the city of nearly 600,000.

So it was quite the surprise when I found myself back in her region, preparing to hold a VBS in the orphanage where she once resided. It was our first full day in the country. The team and I had gone to church and were headed across the square in the city's center toward lunch when a team member said she thought Aksanna, Olya's sister, had just passed us!

I turned in the direction of the passing pedestrians and called out, "Aksanna!"

Right away, a young woman turned around, looking for the person who'd called her name. I began waving my arms wildly so she'd find us. She squinted, unsure of who we were until she got closer. As she realized it was us, a huge smile spread across her face, and she ran to greet us with hugs. She then waved to the young man who was with her (another graduate we knew from the same orphanage), inviting him to join us.

After exchanging a few pleasantries, I asked about Olya. Aksanna pulled out her phone and called her, speaking rapid fire. Moments later, Olya came running up the street, and we embraced and giggled. I couldn't believe God had reunited us!

After chatting for a few moments, I invited the trio to join our team for lunch.

While Olya and I were in line at the blini (crepe) cafe, she said to me (in Russian, of course), "I wore your sweater for a long time."

When she could see that what she was saying didn't register with me, she said, "Sweater . . . sweater . . ."

It wasn't that I didn't understand her words. I just couldn't remember what she was talking about. My mind did furious cartwheels, searching all its files for any memory of a sweater. Then it hit me.

The last day of the last VBS Olya attended at her orphanage, I was torn up about leaving her. Though language rarely flowed smoothly between us, she had been content for most of the week to sit silently at my side, holding my hand. Occasionally, she would show me a photo or participate in a craft, but it was apparent she really just wanted to be near me. That morning, she had been cold and had goosebumps.

I took my sweater off and wrapped it around her shoulders. She smiled broadly, showing her teeth, which were much prettier than most of her compatriots at the children's home. Then she slid her arms into the sleeves.

When it was time to go that afternoon and we were forced to say goodbye, we both had tears in our eyes. She began to take the sweater off to hand it to me. I put my hand up to refuse it. I helped her put it back on and tapped her shoulder to tell her she was to keep it.

Clearly, I had forgotten all about that sweater. Sadly, it was one of too many stuffed into my closet.

When Olya could tell that at last I understood what she was talking about, she continued, "I wore that sweater nearly all the time for so long. It was my favorite. But one day, I saw a girl who lived on the street. She was shivering with cold. I didn't want to give her the sweater, but I understood that she should not be cold. So I gave it to her."

Olya had not been shown much mercy in her life. She'd been abandoned by both of her parents. She hadn't always fit in at the orphanage. Classmates treated her like an outcast. Yet, when faced with the needs of another, Olya chose to show mercy, offering what was precious to her to a stranger.

At this point, I didn't know that Olya was teaching Bible classes to children who still resided in the orphanage or that she was sneaking children out to go to church with her on Sundays, but I was confident she had become a woman of peace, an ambassador of mercy.

Father to the Fatherless

A father to the fatherless, a defender of widows, is God in his holy dwelling. God sets the lonely in families.

PSALM 68:5–6

The first time we visited Pastor Charles's home just outside Bangalore, I asked how he decided to run a children's home. He looked tenderly at his wife and smiled. Then he shared their story.

The couple hadn't always lived in the Bangalore area. During one of Charles's routine three days of prayer and fasting, God told him to move to Karnataka (the state where Bangalore is located). Though he was uncertain what they were to do when they got there, he obeyed. He moved his wife and two daughters to a new and unknown life.

Upon his arrival, Charles met a Korean woman who was in India to build a church. He began assisting her in the building process, figuring it was an appropriate use of his time while he waited for God to convey why he'd been sent to the area. So he worked and prayed and waited for God to reveal His plan.

Before he knew it, the church was completed, and the woman handed the key to him. She said, "God told me to give this to you. Now, you are accountable to Him," and she left. She did not leave an address . . . or even her last name!

Confident that God had shown him what he was to do, Charles began pastoring the church.

The couple was thrilled to be called into ministry, and they began visiting the homes in the area. They offered assistance to those who needed it and invited all to the new church's services.

That wasn't the only blessing the family celebrated. The Lord also gave them a third child, their only son. They rejoiced that he would serve as insurance for their future, as sons do in their culture. They prayed he would grow to be a man of God and serve Him always.

It turned out, God's plans were drastically different from theirs. When he was just five months old, this beloved son died. The death brought an abrupt end to the thrill of their new ministry and ushered in a season of doubt and struggle.

Charles's wife was overcome with grief. She begged her husband to go back to their home and their people. She said she couldn't take the pressure of ministry and the sorrow of missing their son without the support of her family. But when Pastor Charles took this request to the Lord, he received a clear, though undesired, answer: *"Stay. I have greater things for you, things you have not yet imagined."*

Charles apologized to his wife. He empathized with her pain but told her that returning home was not an option. The Lord had spoken, and they would obey.

Just days after this difficult conversation, a knock came on their door. When they opened it, a neighbor was standing on the step with a baby boy in her arms. There had been an accident, she explained, and the boy's parents were dead. "Would you Christians take him?"

Charles and his wife eagerly agreed. They named the boy Nathan and committed to raising Him to know God Almighty as his Lord. While not a replacement for the son they lost, they recognized that Nathan was another blessing from the Lord.

Today, Charles's family is not short on blessings. You see, word spread in that neighborhood that the Christians would take children who needed a home. So each time illness or abuse or addiction struck, the youngest victims were carried directly to the church built by a Korean woman, the one where Charles and his wife had committed to stay, the one with more children than grown-ups and more laughter than tears.

When we last visited, Pastor Charles and his wife shared their approximately 120-square-foot room with their two daughters and twelve orphans. They not only provide for the children's needs but also treasure an emotional bond with them, as well. By surrendering to God's will, Charles had become a father to the fatherless, just like the God he serves.

Questions to Ponder or Discuss

Before reading chapter three, read Romans 12:12 and consider: How can patience in affliction be lived out?

After reading the chapter:

1) Is there anyone you're struggling to forgive? What can this chapter offer you as a help?

2) Has anyone ever given you a gift that meant far more than its material value? What was it, and why did it mean so much to you?

3) Do you know anyone who's become a father to the fatherless? Maybe it was a legal adoption; maybe it was in the form of a mentor. What impact did that person make on the life of the individual being cared for?

CHAPTER 4

Covenant

HOW TO BE ASSURED YOUR PRAYERS
ARE HEARD

I stood, staring at the plain wall in front of me—big, salty tears rolling down my face.

I had prayed before for walls to come *down*, from the formidable Berlin Wall to the less tangible barriers between family members. But never in my life had I been so thankful for a wall to be constructed!

It was 2006, and we had already been working in this particular orphanage for six years. We had brought many volunteers to the orphanage to conduct Vacation Bible Schools or construction projects. Nearly all left with a specific burden for the children of this particular village orphanage. We'll call it Orphanage X.

According to many orphanage directors in the region, children who do not fare well in other orphanages were sent to Orphanage X. The result was a "home" where hazing and pack mentality reigned.

It was clear the unthinkable happened at night.

Because this was a state-run institution, we had no authority to make staffing decisions. We *could* continue to send volunteers into the orphanage to build relationships and share Christ, but it was a difficult environment for that.

A Boaz Project team in 2005 got an especially clear picture of the horrors that were commonplace in Orphanage X.

There were girls who could not make eye contact and dodged the presence of boys. There were teens who bore signs of cutting and alcohol abuse. There were littler ones whose food was being taken from them.

Though we saw so many signs of abuse and cruelty, one situation startled us all. On our second day of Vacation Bible School in this particular orphanage, the "gaishniki," or police, returned two boys who had attempted to run away. I was outside when the police left but could soon hear the boys crying out from inside the orphanage as they were beaten.

One of our team members ran inside and tore up the stairs, prepared to defend the boys, whatever the cost. At his appearance, the beating stopped.

The next day, we could not find the two boys. When asked, the orphanage staff simply stated that they were being punished for running away and would not be joining us for games and crafts.

That afternoon, we noticed some children speaking in hushed tones in the hallway, hurriedly gathering around a door and then scattering as quickly. We eventually understood that the two teens were in that room, stripped naked, left in isolation. They remained there the rest of the week, locked in and stripped of their clothes so that another escape was not possible.

Seeing the harsh reality of these children's lives shook our team, and they committed to pray—not just while they were in Russia, but daily, faithfully after they returned home to the States.

It was about six weeks after we departed from Russia that we learned that the director of that orphanage had been replaced. You have to understand: this was a miracle!

As government-appointed positions, most orphanage director posts remain filled until the designee faces death or retirement. And the now-former director didn't appear to be close to either. Yet, without explanation, she was no longer the director of Orphanage X. I'm confident it was because our team had moved mighty forces in the heavenly realms.

Within a month of the new director taking the position, she asked our administrator if she could use some of the funds we had pledged to build a wall. It was a request we had not received before.

She explained that she had divided the girls' rooms from the boys' rooms, putting them on opposite ends of the hallway. But she needed a wall to separate the two ends.

Of course, we answered with an immediate and enthusiastic, "Yes!"

And so, when I returned to Orphanage X just a few months later, I saw a wall. A wall that protected frightened girls who were unaccustomed to being able to sleep at night. A wall that represented a new regime in the orphanage. A wall built by the desperate prayers of our teams and of the children.

We could not march into the orphanage, hammers and nails in hand, and just begin building a wall. We could not demand that they build a wall. We could not petition for a wall. We had no authority to do so. From an earthly perspective, we were powerless, unable to protect the children we knew were suffering.

From a spiritual perspective, however, we had the only resource we needed: admission to the very throne room of God. Our team knew that prayer is our most valuable tool for accessing the resources of heaven when doing kingdom work, and they employed it.

> *Prayer is our most valuable tool for accessing the resources of heaven when doing kingdom work.*

Prayer Insurance

Of course, our prayers are not always answered according to our expectations. Sometimes the wait is much longer than we'd like. Sometimes our hopes for a loved one's healing or change of heart appear to have no substance. Sometimes we get discouraged and are tempted to give up on prayer, having seen no fruit for the time and emotional energy invested imploring God for intervention. It can appear as though there's some "secret sauce" or magic wording or perfect posture required for God to hear our prayers—some special trick that we don't know.

Funny thing is, there is!

Now before you toss this book aside with cries of, "Heresy!" hear me out.

You see, once upon a time, the Israelites felt the same way. Foreigners had burned their city and beaten their citizens. Their fields were ravaged by oppressors. The whole country was desolate. It's fair to say that times were tough.

Of course, the Israelites were praying—beseeching even—to no avail. They were offering burnt sacrifices in an attempt to draw God's attention to their plight. They burned incense. According to the book of Isaiah, they made a multitude of sacrifices and held convocations. But their prayers for God's protection, their longings for His provision, their claims of His promises rendered nothing.

Despite the Israelites' designation as God's chosen people, despite their flaunting of sacrifices and incense, despite their pleas for mercy, God did not answer their prayers. In fact, in Isaiah 1:15, God says: "When you spread out your hands in prayer, I hide my eyes from you; even when you offer many prayers, I am not listening."

Ouch! That's not something I ever want to hear God say! How terrifying to consider that God could choose to ignore my prayers, my cries for help.

Why was God so far off?

God answered this question in verse 17 of the same chapter (we looked at this verse in chapter two, as well) when He instructs the Israelites, "Learn to do right; seek justice. Defend the oppressed. Take up the cause of the fatherless; plead the case of the widow."

Did you catch that, friend? God was not answering the prayers of the Israelites in their dark hour because they were not seeking justice for their fellow man. They were not defending the oppressed. They were not fighting on behalf of the orphan or the widow.

The remedy was not more sacrifices of fattened calves. It was seeking solace for the fatherless child. God didn't want more incense or genuflections; He wanted more insistence on justice.

> *God doesn't want more incense or genuflections; He wants more insistence on justice.*

The Almighty then goes on to promise His children that if they turn from their hardened hearts and care for the widow and orphan, He will answer the prayers they have uttered in distress. He will forgive their sins and defend them against their oppressors.

Of course, I'm not saying that caring for the orphan and widow creates some kind of magic wand that puts God at our bidding. His ways are still higher than our ways and His thoughts are still higher than ours (Isaiah 55:9). We may not understand—or like—why God answers our petitions the way in which He does. But He has promised us that when we care for the poor and oppressed, He hears our prayers and answers them.

Lest you think I'm stretching the Scriptures, let's look at another example. In Isaiah 58, God's people ask for His decisions, for Him to come near. In verse three, they ask: "'Why have we fasted?' they say, 'and you have not seen it? Why have we humbled ourselves, and you have not noticed?'"

Can you feel their frustration? They're seeking ways to petition God, even depriving themselves of nourishment! Yet the Everlasting Father seems distant from them.

Their Counselor has not moved. He is not deaf, and He isn't dependent upon His children's fasting. No, His lack of response to their rituals and cries is based on their lack of concern for the voiceless. He explains it this way in verses 6–9:

> "Is not this the kind of fasting I have chosen: to loose the chains of injustice and untie the cords of the yoke, to set the oppressed free and break every yoke? Is it not to share your food with the hungry and to provide the poor wanderer with shelter— when you see the naked, to clothe them, and not to turn away from your own flesh and blood? Then your light will break forth like the dawn, and your healing will quickly appear; then your righteousness will go before you, and the glory of the LORD will be your rear guard. Then you will call, and the LORD will answer; you will cry for help, and he will say: Here am I."

More than any display of discipline, God honors your ministry to the marginalized.

This same concept is laid out for us in Zechariah chapter 7. Zechariah, a prophet, asks God on behalf of the people if they should participate in their regularly scheduled fast. God replies, saying that they hadn't really been fasting for Him as much as for their own credit. So He admonishes them in verses 9–10: "This is what the LORD Almighty said: 'Administer

More than any display of discipline, God honors your ministry to the marginalized.

true justice; show mercy and compassion to one another. Do not oppress the widow or the fatherless, the foreigner or the poor. Do not plot evil against each other.'"

So once again, God shows a preference for justice, mercy, and compassion over ritualistic fasting.

True to the haughty nature God accused them of, the Israelites decide to fast anyway. I suppose that's easier than administering justice, and maybe they figured it would get them a few brownie points anyway.

It did not.

In fact, verse 12 says it made the Lord Almighty "very angry." He explains it this way in verses 13–14:

> "'When I called, they did not listen; so when they called, I would not listen,' says the LORD Almighty. 'I scattered them with a whirlwind among all the nations, where they were strangers. The land they left behind them was so desolate that no one traveled through it. This is how they made the pleasant land desolate.'"

Yes, I'd say that's very angry!

The people had been warned. God had explained how to regain His favor. He basically told them to get their acts together and care for those who were being taken advantage of in their society. Yet their commitment to a lifestyle of oppressing the widow, the orphan, the foreigner, and the poor was so great that it ended up costing them everything. Because when they called, God did not listen.

Friends, prayer is too valuable an asset to forfeit. Let's live in such a way that our heavenly Father is eager to hear and answer us. I'm not saying we can earn God's favor or do certain deeds to get our way through the pearly gates. But I do think

Prayer is too valuable an asset to forfeit.

the Scriptures we've just examined demonstrate a correlation between how we treat the exploited and how He responds to our prayers.

The prayers uttered for the children of Orphanage X by that short-term team were born out of true care for orphans. Those team members had visited orphans, as instructed in James 1:27. They had allowed the orphans they met to penetrate their hearts. They carried their requests on behalf of those children to the throne room faithfully. They had fulfilled their side of this covenant. And God fulfilled His!

Of course, when you're truly burdened for those overlooked by the rest of society, you're typically not praying with this arrangement in mind, "Since I care for the marginalized, God will answer my prayers!" You just pray for them because it's the natural thing to do.

God Knows Best

I'll offer our prayers for Vika as another example.

As many do, this story begins with our family and a short-term team of volunteers holding a Vacation Bible School in a Russian orphanage. My children were probably in grades five and seven at this time, so they were assigned to groups as helpers. Though they didn't lead the groups, their familiarity with the orphanages put them at ease and enabled them to interact with the children freely.

Well, on this particular trip, our daughter was assigned to a group of six- and seven-year-olds. Halfway through the first day, I visited the group to see how they were getting along.

"Watch, Mom!" Berea blurted out.

I stopped by the tiny yellow table where she was seated. She took a crayon, placed it on the table, and it began rolling off because the table was so lopsided. Just as it fell from the edge, Berea placed her hand underneath and caught it. The little piggy-tailed girl next to her burst out in laughter. The laugh was so contagious, I giggled as well.

Berea returned the crayon to its starting position and allowed it to roll once again, only to be caught mid-fall. The six-year-old cutie next to her cackled again.

"I've been doing this over and over," Berea marveled, "and she still thinks it's funny!"

I learned that the little girl's name was Vika. She was sweet as could be, and her amusement at the rolling and catching of the crayon continued for quite some time.

"She doesn't talk," Berea added matter-of-factly.

The weight of those words was not lost on me.

Berea had been her brother, Noah's, mouthpiece for many years. He'd been in speech therapy and occupational therapy. He'd had devices to correct the structure of his mouth and lessons in sign language. Therapists actually thought he'd never speak.

Thanks to God's intervention, no one who knows Noah today would ever guess that he once struggled to put intelligible sound to his thoughts. But the history left us with an understanding, an empathy for others facing the same challenges.

I was thankful Berea wasn't daunted by the little girl's inability to communicate and that she was offering her some precious one-on-one attention and levity.

The next day, as our team was preparing to head to the orphanage, Berea asked me, "Can Noah come to my group today?"

I usually tried to separate my children into different groups so none of the team felt like they were actually babysitting Americans while they were in Russia and so that they would not have to deal with any sibling quarrels. They were getting older now, though, so I considered her request.

I began my research into the matter by asking, "Why do you want him in your group today?"

"Because I want him to meet Vika. I think they'd get along," she replied.

It was a difficult request to refuse, so I allowed the change-up.

When I entered the group midmorning, Berea, Noah, and Vika were throwing poorly made paper airplanes for short distances. It was their spirits that really soared that day; they enjoyed one another's silliness so thoroughly.

At some point during the week, I asked the director about Vika. I learned that she had a condition called phenylketonuria, which basically meant she lacked an enzyme that breaks down proteins. She was kept to a strict special diet and had to drink a glass full of a thick, white substance each morning.

The lack of speech was an unrelated issue, but a formidable one.

When we returned home, our children continued to speak of Vika. They'd remember pulling her on a sled or watching her blow bubbles. They put a picture she had colored on our refrigerator and prayed for her each bedtime. They'd met so many children before, but this one had worked her way into their hearts like none other. Occasionally, they'd suggest we adopt her.

When it was time to return to Vika's region of Russia, both of our children began requesting that they be placed in her group. And they began mentioning adoption more frequently and fervently.

A joyous reunion was celebrated by Vika, Berea, and Noah. The three spent the week together, taking selfies, coloring, and giggling. Jim and I watched and contemplated.

Midweek, I visited the group as the children were getting bundled to go outside. They had stepped into the cloakroom to prepare for the snowy weather while I waited in their main room. Vika was the first to come back, donning her coat, hat, and mittens. She was jumping with excitement, eager to play.

"Gatovy? Gatova! (You guys ready? I'm ready!)" she called toward the others.

I quickly looked around. Were there no other witnesses? Vika just spoke! There was no one else here. It had to be her! And it was so clear.

I made my way to the director's office. "Can Vika talk now?" I asked.

"No," the director replied. "We often try to coax her, but she just isn't able."

No one else had witnessed the phenomena, but I knew what I had heard. Vika had spoken. Her lack of speech, I came to believe, was not an inability, but a response to her environment. I held onto the hope that the child would one day speak again.

The week in Vika's orphanage passed too quickly, and once again we found ourselves headed for home.

Somehow, Vika became a part of our daily conversation, even while separated by an ocean and more.

On the way to school each morning, as I prayed over my kids' day, we'd pray for Vika, too. We added a picture of her to her artwork that hung on the fridge. The kids often talked about what they'd do together when they'd see her again. And they continued to insist that she belonged in our family.

Though we had concerns about our ability to provide everything Vika needed, we began to entertain the idea of adopting her. I'd had to work with special diets before. We had been prepared already to raise a child who couldn't speak. Perhaps it was all in preparation for Vika.

So when we found ourselves in Vika's orphanage once again, we inquired.

It turned out that another family was already in the process of adopting Vika. Americans, we were told. They'd been to Russia once already to meet her. The director appeared confident it was a good family and that they'd be able to provide whatever medical care or therapy she may need.

I knew it was good news, but I also knew it would be hard to convince my children of that.

"And another thing . . ." the director added, "She can talk. She just started one day, in full sentences."

"Vika's being adopted!" I exclaimed to my children in the most positive tone I could muster, "by a family that can give her everything she needs."

Their faces fell.

Jim and I encouraged them to trust God's plan and to pray for Vika's new family.

Berea and Noah soaked up those days with Vika, sliding down slides, playing in a sandbox, and listening to Bible stories. The goodbye was difficult at the end of the week, as each of the children knew it was final.

It was hard to know how to handle the situation. Of course, we knew it was right to continue to pray for Vika. But to have her picture and artwork hanging in our kitchen began to feel somehow disrespectful of her new family. She was headed home now, and we needed to embrace God's plan for her. Having prayed for this child so much, we had no choice but to trust that God had answered in the way that was best.

We still occasionally spoke of Vika, but not as frequently as before. We prayed, but the prayers were for a family and a world we knew nothing about. We wondered how she was doing and prayed that her new family loved Jesus.

Things were even more awkward when we returned to Vika's orphanage, but she wasn't there. Of course, we interacted with the other children, but it simply wasn't the same.

A couple years after that last trip with Vika, I was at the office when my phone rang. When I answered it, a young woman I consider to be like a daughter was on the other end. "Are you near your computer?" she asked before even saying hello.

I affirmed that I was, and she gave me a web address. I typed it in, and an adoption blog came up on my screen. "Isn't that Vika?" Jessi asked.

"Oh my word. It is! How . . . ? Wha . . ." was all I could muster.

Jessi jumped in. "I was researching other families' adoption experiences in that region as we prepare for ours. I was reading this one when I saw the picture, and it hit me that I knew her! She was the girl on your refrigerator!"

By that afternoon, I was talking on the phone with Vika's mother.

She was precious! She was eager to hear stories of her daughter from the days before they met. She recounted their adoption story, how God had led them to add to their family. She bragged on her daughter's adjustment to the family and to the US. Vika was not only speaking, but in English! She could read among the top students in her class, and she loved to sing.

I didn't want to scare the sweet woman by telling her how very much we loved her daughter. I didn't want her to think we'd creep or kidnap or something. Instead, I promised pictures we had taken on our visits and expressed my joy that Vika was so happy.

I told her about our work in Russia's orphanages as justification for our knowledge of Vika. She excitedly responded that it explained Vika's knowledge of the Bible. From the time she began speaking English, she was asserting "Jesus loves me!" and retelling Bible stories! Her mother expressed her gratitude for investing in the lives of Russia's orphans and in her daughter.

I ventured far enough to tell her that Vika had a special place in our hearts, and she understood, fully aware that her daughter is special indeed. I also confided that we had been praying for her daily.

When asked about medical care and therapies, Vika's mom responded, "It's really miraculous. She hasn't needed any!"

I was stunned. The phenylketonuria was probably the reason she'd been abandoned at birth. But it didn't exist?

I must have said something about Russia's rate of misdiagnoses, because I remember being humbled when she replied, "Oh, no! I believe the diagnosis was accurate. It was your family's faithful prayers before we even knew Vika that healed her!"

Whoa. Could that be? Is it possible that God bound our hearts to Vika's so tightly so that we would be moved to pray consistently, fervently for her?

My theology says yes. Yes, God would bring our family around the world repeatedly to endear a child to our hearts. Yes, God would heal a child in response to our family's prayers. Yes, God would then place that child in the home that He knows is the perfect fit. And yes, every once in a while—just to display His glory—He would allow the two families to meet and marvel at Him.

And based on the Scriptures we've examined in this chapter, I'd say the prayers for Vika were bolstered because they were birthed out of love for the defenseless and abandoned.

> *James 5:16 tells us that the prayers of the righteous are "powerful and effective."*

James 5:16 tells us that the prayers of the righteous are "powerful and effective." Certainly that doesn't mean those prayers are always answered in the way we want. But it does mean they're answered in the way that is best. And sometimes, we get a glimpse of God's glory in the process.

Questions to Ponder or Discuss

Before reading chapter four, read Isaiah 55:9. Do you like the fact that God's ways are higher than ours? Why or why not?

After reading the chapter:

1) Share a miraculous answer to prayer you've witnessed.

2) When have you seen a prayer answered in a completely different way than you anticipated?

3) Which passage from this chapter spoke to you most? Why?

CHAPTER 5

Companionship

HOW GOD MEETS YOUR GREATEST NEEDS

The ringing of the phone startled me awake. A panic set in as I wondered why someone was calling at that hour.

"Hello?" I managed to form the word.

"April!" the caller replied. "I'm so sorry to call. I know it's the middle of the night there, but we just don't know what to do!"

As my brain began functioning, I pieced the situation together. My dear friend was in Russia. She and her husband had gone to complete their adoption and bring their son home. She was calling because meeting him hadn't gone exactly as planned, and the couple feared they may be unable to care for him.

I could hear the desperation in her voice. They had wanted this child for so long, had prayed for him and looked forward to holding him. They had completed

frequently yield detrimental consequences for a child at some point in her life.[1] The more prolonged the traumatic event(s), the more severe the damage it causes.

To combat the dangers associated with trauma, neuroscientists, therapists, and attachment specialists agree unanimously: a child needs a safe and loving caregiver.

God did not create us—especially children—to function independent of community. Rather, He designed us to require relationship and interaction so that we would recognize our need for Him. He placed other humans in our lives as models, examples from whom we could learn to interact socially. Life without those relationships proves detrimental to our development in every way.

> *To combat the dangers associated with trauma, neuroscientists, therapists, and attachment specialists agree unanimously: a child needs a safe and loving caregiver.*

I believe God created us with this innate need for relationship because He desires to fulfill it. So throughout human history, He has given us physical manifestations of His presence.

[1] Illinois Childhood Trauma Coalition, "What Is Childhood Trauma?" Looking Through Their Eyes, http://lookthroughtheireyes.org/what-is-childhood-trauma/; Bruce D. Perry, MD, PhD, *Stress, Trauma, and Post-Traumatic Stress Disorders in Children: An Introduction*, The ChildTrauma Academy, https://childtrauma.org/wp-content/uploads/2013/11/PTSD_Caregivers.pdf; Bruce Perry, interview by Oprah Winfrey, "Treating Childhood Trauma," *60 Minutes*, March 11, 2018, 4:15–5:20 and 5:40–6:38, https://www.cbsnews.com/news/oprah-winfrey-treating-childhood-trauma/.

Prior to the fall, when creation remained perfect, God walked in the Garden of Eden alongside Adam and Eve. His presence was physical and unmistakable.

After mankind was banned from the Garden, God began sending prophets to communicate and interact on His behalf.

When His people were fleeing Egypt to head to the Promised Land, God became a pillar of cloud by day and a pillar of fire by night, just to reassure His people that He was with them.

Then God's Spirit took up residency in the transportable tabernacle and, eventually, the more permanent Temple.

In due time, God sent His Son, Jesus, to walk the earth. He was the Divine made human. He showed us God's character and became the sacrifice that justified us.

Today, He fills each of us who believe in Him for our salvation with His Holy Spirit. He is ever present in us.

According to John 14:23, "Jesus replied, 'Anyone who loves me will obey my teaching. My Father will love them, and we will come to them and make our home with them.'"

The Trinity makes its home in us! The Father, Son, and Holy Spirit come to stay, assuring us they are always present. Thus, God fulfills our greatest need.

The Trinity makes its home in us!

Oh, we long for Him to see us through our trials. We even ask Him to meet specific material needs. But really, what our souls long for most is His presence.

Perhaps this is why Jesus promises us in John 14:18, "I will not leave you as orphans; I will come to you."

Notice that He doesn't say here that He'll feed or clothe us. He doesn't mention education or wide social circles. He doesn't promise to grant wishes like some kind of genie. But He does promise to come to us, to be present with us, to satisfy our greatest need.

I'll confess that sometimes I want the genie. I want a quick fix to my dilemma. I want to be spared heartache. I want to zip through seasons of waiting and know God's answer on the front-end. I want my friends to be healed, my children to be happy.

Yet God gives us something greater—the opportunity and responsibility to grow more like Him. And He promises to be with us as we go through it all.

Elisha

Often, when I meet a child who's new to one of our partner homes, the caregivers will brief me on the circumstances that brought him to the home. They fill me in on whether or not the child's birth date is known, the whereabouts of any living relatives, and how he's adjusted to his new surroundings. This was the case when I first met Elisha in Kenya.

Elisha, I was told, has two brothers and three sisters. One day, while the children were preparing dinner, their mother added poison to the food, apparently planning to kill all six children at once.

I could hardly fathom the words I was hearing. How could a mother do such a thing to any child, let alone her flesh and blood? How could she knowingly bring them harm? It is a violation of God and of nature for a woman to turn on her own.

Yet this is the kind of trauma so many children endure, and the scarring is more than physical. This experience taught Elisha he could not trust anyone. He took to the streets to fend for himself, a job no child should have.

Thankfully, God created our brains and spirits with the ability to heal, just as He did our skin and bones.

Attachment Cycle

In a healthy environment, parents take seriously the responsibility of tending to their child's needs, comforting them in their fears or pain, and communicating safety and love. This innate compulsion is a necessary part of what attachment therapists refer to as the attachment cycle.[2]

It looks like this: A newborn is hungry, and so he cries. A mother recognizes his need and feeds him. He is calmed until he is in need of a diaper change, at which point he cries again. Dad sees the problem and changes the diaper. All is well in the little family until baby has another need, at which point, he cries.

This rhythmic pattern of need emerging, need communicating, and need meeting continue day after day (and night after night!). Over time, the child learns that his parents are available, capable, and trustworthy. So he continues to communicate his needs with them.

This cycle of behaviors is more than just a means of a child getting the food and attention she needs, however. It is actually crucial to her physical, cognitive, and social development.

---

[2] Christa Nelson, "What Is Healthy Attachment?" *Our Voices* (blog), May 18, 2014, www.attachmenttraumanetwork.org/what-is-healthy-attachment/.

In fact, without the critical attachment to an adult, children are likely to suffer from learning disabilities, anxiety, chemical imbalances, sensory disorders, stunted growth, and more. Often, this can be traced back to elevated levels of cortisol in infants and children who are not nurtured by a loving adult. Intellectual potential is also minimized, as the child's brain is too preoccupied with matters of survival—like food, sleep, and safety—to entertain thinking on higher levels.

Many children from trauma don't know who will take care of them. Abandonment, abuse, or extreme poverty prematurely set them on a course of independence. If a child is hungry, he must steal or beg to provide for himself. If he gets hurt, he must soldier on.

These same risk factors make children all the more likely to enter the sex trade. Not only are they without defense against perpetrators, but they are also lured by a pimp's promise that they will be fed and clothed. You see, it's not just the food and clothes that are attractive. It is the promise. It is the someone who makes the promise. It is the willingness of that someone to take away the hardship of providing for oneself. It is attachment. This desperate, innate desire for a child to satisfy her basic needs can lure her into dangerous situations.

If removed from an environment of abuse and neglect, it is possible for a child to heal. It is not a quick fix, a guaranteed outcome, or an easy road. It takes effort and time from multiple parties. Therapeutic counseling, academic support, and firm boundaries all support the necessary rewiring of the brain that needs to take place after a child experiences trauma. Yet attachment therapists maintain that the single most important ingredient in helping a traumatized child become a healthy, productive member of society is the presence of a safe and loving adult who will respond to his needs.[3]

Much of the training we offer house parents and volunteers centers around this issue of helping a child step down from his hypervigilant state of self-protection by building trust and security. We assure him that his needs will be met by loving caregivers.

Thankfully, Elisha's new caregivers were faithful to meet his needs. Over time, he has begun to trust that some adults can be consistently kind. They can be depended upon for provision and nurturing. They can want what's best for him.

What about Us?

It is true that—through His presence in our lives—God meets our greatest need. But He doesn't stop there. He tends to us day by day and moment by moment to ensure our every need is met. Christ offered us this assurance in Matthew 6:25–34:

> "Therefore I tell you, do not worry about your life, what you will eat or drink; or about your body, what you will wear. Is not life more than food, and the body more than clothes? Look at the birds of

---

[3] Bruce Perry, interview by Oprah Winfrey, "Treating Childhood Trauma," *60 Minutes*, March 11, 2018, 12:14–12:54, https://www.cbsnews.com/news/oprah-winfrey-treating-childhood-trauma/; Nicole Wilke, Meredith Morgan, and Alisha Pangborn, *The Changing Brain: Created to Heal* (Christian Alliance for Orphans, 2018), 18, 26, https://issuu.com/christianalliancefororphans/docs/the_changing_brain_single_page.

the air; they do not sow or reap or store away in barns, and yet your heavenly Father feeds them. Are you not much more valuable than they? Can any one of you by worrying add a single hour to your life?

"And why do you worry about clothes? See how the flowers of the field grow. They do not labor or spin. Yet I tell you that not even Solomon in all his splendor was dressed like one of these. If that is how God clothes the grass of the field, which is here today and tomorrow is thrown into the fire, will he not much more clothe you—you of little faith? So do not worry, saying, 'What shall we eat?' or 'What shall we drink?' or 'What shall we wear?' For the pagans run after all these things, and your heavenly Father knows that you need them. But seek first his kingdom and his righteousness, and all these things will be given to you as well. Therefore do not worry about tomorrow, for tomorrow will worry about itself. Each day has enough trouble of its own."

We were created with needs for food and shelter and sleep. According to this passage, however, that isn't cause for alarm. Our heavenly Father knows our needs and takes care of them.

> *Our heavenly Father knows our needs and takes care of them.*

He's a good Father, performing His role in the attachment cycle. He hears our cries and answers them. He knows our needs and provides them. He is always present, always attentive, always capable of tending to our needs.

It's comforting to have such a Provider because, really, it's about more than our need for food and clothing. It's the promise. It is the Someone who makes the promise. It is the willingness of that Someone to take away the hardship of providing for oneself. It is attachment. This desperate, innate desire to satisfy my basic needs can drive me deeper into relationship with my heavenly Father if I only trust Him with it.

Questions to Ponder or Discuss

Before reading chapter five, read John 14:23. What does it mean to you to "make your home" with someone?

After reading the chapter:

1) When have you just wanted someone near? Someone who's not trying to fix your problem or alter your mood but just sit with you in it?

2) Can you tell of a time when you endured a situation you wanted to escape, only to see God refining you through it?

3) How have you seen God meet a material need in a miraculous fashion?

CHAPTER 6

Connection

HOW GOD STRATEGICALLY PURSUES
RELATIONSHIP WITH YOU

"What's wrong?" I worried. I headed toward the boys to find out, but an orphanage worker put her hand on my arm to stop me.

We were visiting a rural orphanage in Russia, and some of the team had gone outside to play with the children. As I exited the building to check on them, I saw two boys, their backs turned to me, waving wildly and jumping up and down. It looked like a movie scene where someone stranded on a deserted island tries to get the attention of a plane overhead.

"It's their parents," the orphanage worker explained.

Confused, I continued walking toward the boys, but at a slower pace. A team member stepped toward me, "They did this yesterday, too," she whispered.

"Did what? What are they doing?" I asked.

"Trying to get their parents' attention. That's them . . . on the balcony," my teammate answered.

I looked up in the direction the boys were facing, and there, on the balcony three stories up, was a couple, smoking and chatting.

I soon learned that this was a daily—if not more frequent—routine. The parents would come to their balcony overlooking the orphanage grounds to smoke. The sons would try desperately to get their parents' attention; the parents would refuse to even glance in their direction. And yet, the next time they stepped outside, the boys would be there, watching and waving.

Eye Contact

This scene in the orphanage yard exposed the need each of us has to be seen, to be noticed, to be important to someone. It's an innate craving that must be satisfied or we will be consumed by its lack. We'll try new methods of getting attention until something works. We'll create a scene until we're seen.

We'll create a scene until we're seen.

From birth we have this need, this desire for acknowledgment, this search for eye contact.

You'll understand what I mean if you visit YouTube and search "still face experiment." There, you'll see videos of Dr. Edward Tronick, the director of the Child Development Unit at the University of Massachusetts Boston, conduct telling research with infants and their mothers.

It begins with mothers playfully interacting with their

little ones. But things change when the mothers—as part of the experiment—go straight-faced and unresponsive.

Baby after cooing baby, moods change when Mom stops interacting. Suddenly, the cheeriest little cherubs become sullen and sulk. They'll cry, point, or wave to get some attention. The longer the mother is able to hold out without returning her attention to her child, the more dramatic the wee one's attempts to get her to do so. In a period of minutes, the babies go from irritated to desperate.

For children who've known extended neglect, this lack of attention has become the norm. Attempts at attracting attention may have become extreme or may have completely ceased due to their futility.

This is why attachment therapists will emphasize the importance of making eye contact as a means of establishing a bond with a child who's known trauma. The act of letting a child know he is seen, interesting, and worthy of attention is critical for beginning a healing process. It may take time before the child is even comfortable meeting eyes with her caregiver, but the loving adult will pursue connection through eye contact.[1]

Perhaps this is why David implores the Lord in Psalm 102:2, "Do not hide your face from me." He can face a lot of troubles but not the loss of God's attention. He needs the intimacy, the reassurance that God sees him. In fact, in the New American Standard version of the Bible, David asks five times in his psalms for God to shine His face upon him or "upon us."

---

[1] Karyn Purvis, David R. Cross, and Wendy Lyons Sunshine, *The Connected Child: Bring Hope and Healing to Your Adoptive Family* (New York: McGraw-Hill Education, 2007), 78, 144–145.

Hagar also relished being seen by God.

Genesis 16 and 17 tell us that her life had not been simple. She was a maidservant (not the most prestigious position). When her mistress, Sarai, arranged for her to spend the night with Abraham in order to bear a son, it became the source of irritation between the two women. So Hagar ran away. On her own, jobless, and homeless, desperation had surely set in.

When God blessed Hagar with a child—and even sent an angel to her to chat about the pregnancy—she gave God a new name. She called Him "The God Who Sees Me."

What was important to Hagar? Not that God had fed her, not that He had given her a child—not even that the angel had promised her a multitude of offspring. What Hagar marveled in was that God had *seen* her. He knew her dire circumstances and intervened. He noticed. He cared enough to see.

Let me assure you, friend, that God sees you, too.

First Peter 3:12 tells us that "the eyes of the Lord are on the righteous." Now, I realize you may not see yourself as righteous, but if you've accepted Christ's sacrifice on your behalf, that's exactly what you are. He's made you righteous, blameless before God. Therefore, God keeps His eye on you!

In the same way that a loving adult seeks to attach with a hurting child, God wants you to feel attached to Him. Even when His gaze is uncomfortable for you, your loving Father will pursue this

> *God sees you, and His gaze is never taken from you.*

connection. He longs for the day when you turn your focus to Him.

God sees you, and His gaze is never taken from you.

Obey Authority

As powerful as eye contact is for forming a bond with a child, it is not the only method recommended by attachment therapists. There are many. In the remainder of this chapter, I'd like to discuss some of them.

Most therapists will agree that it's important for children—especially children from trauma—to learn to respect and obey authority. This is not in order to give some power trip to the adult, as some adults fear. Rather, knowing that someone else, someone older, wiser, and hopefully kind is in charge frees the child from a lot of worry and stress. It frees the child to, well, be a child.

Without this authority figure, the child desperately seeks to control a world of chaos. When he is unable, he scrounges for new means: manipulation, lies, temper tantrums, self-harm, or even violating others. He'll stop at nothing.

When it comes to helping such children, Jayne Schooler is an expert. She's the author of *Wounded Children, Healing Homes: How Traumatized Children Impact Foster and Adoptive Families*. I've been fortunate to take part in several seminars and workshops in which Jayne was the trainer. I can't say we're friends, but Jayne's the kind of warm, approachable person who makes everyone feel like she's a friend. (That explains why I went all fangirl when I saw a main character reading the aforementioned book on *This is Us*!)

Jayne bases her methodology for parenting children from hard places on a concept of "Anchor and Orientation." She teaches that you must first be an anchor for children, a firm foundation that makes them feel secure. Then you provide their orientation by showing them which way to go. You guide them into right behaviors and choices.

Part of this process includes establishing the authority of the parent. The resulting security for a child can yield profound improvements in her self-worth, her behavior, and her perception of the world around her. She learns the boundaries set by the adult and finds peaceful freedom inside them.

That's why God's Word instructs parents in Proverbs 22:6 to "start children off on the way they should go," and promises that, "even when they are old they will not turn from it." Anchor them, then be their compass, their life GPS. There may be some "rerouting" along the way as children learn to trust, but we can give them the direction they need to get off to a good start.

Do you know that God plays this role for us, too? Isaiah 30:21 promises us so. It's addressing the wayward Israelites, commanding them to listen to God's voice and obey Him. It quotes God, saying, "Whether you turn to the right or to the left, your ears will hear a voice behind you, saying, 'This is the way; walk in it.'"

Later, in chapter 48, Isaiah wrote, "This is what the LORD says—your Redeemer, the Holy One of Israel: 'I am the LORD your God, who teaches you what is best for you, who directs you in the way you should go'" (v. 17). This authority is not in order to give God some power trip, as some folks fear. Rather, knowing that someone else, someone older, wiser, and truly kind is in charge should free us from a lot of worry and stress. It frees us to, well, be His children!

David put it this way in Psalm 32:8: "I will instruct you and teach you in the way you should go; I will counsel you with my loving eye on you." When God provides us with direction and purpose, we should not fear obedience. Rather, we can trust that His counsel is offered with His loving eye on us! He is looking out for our best interests, our growth, our joy. He is benevolently giving us the guidance we need for abundant life.

Psalm 119:105 reinforces this concept: "Your Word is a lamp for my feet, a light on my path." God's consistently showing us which way to go.

God is our anchor, our security, the firmest of foundations. He also—through His Word and His Holy Spirit—gives us our direction, our orientation.

God is our anchor, our security, the firmest of foundations.

In fact, Jesus claims to be that path we should take. Catch what He told His disciples, as recorded in John 14:6: "I am the way and the truth and the life. No one comes to the Father except through me." All the direction and orientation we could need is summed up in the person of Jesus. He's the way! Seek Him, follow Him, move toward Him, and you will arrive at the destination God ordained for you.

Without accepting God's authority in our lives, we'll desperately seek to control a world of chaos. When we're unable, we'll scrounge for new means: manipulation, lies, temper tantrums, self-harm, or even violating others. We'll stop at nothing.

If, on the other hand, we accept the boundaries God set for us and embrace the path He set us on, we will note profound improvements in our self-worth, our behaviors, and our perceptions of the world around us. We'll find a peaceful freedom inside God's will.

Offer Children a Voice

What's your favorite color?

For most of us, that's a pretty simple question to answer. Many orphaned children, however, cannot.

Institutional life leaves little room for individuality. No one gets to have a special cup, a specific chair, or a preferred way to wear their hair. No one chooses when to get up in the morning, how long they can linger over lunch, or which book will be read to them, if any. Rather, life is a regimented, collective routine. No choices are offered and, therefore, no choices are made.

An attachment therapist would tell you that's not ideal. A child should learn how to make choices and voice opinions. She should gain confidence in her ability to make decisions by occasionally having the power to do so. It may be about which colored cup to drink from for lunch today, but that will assist in her making more significant choices tomorrow.

She should be permitted to speak about her day, her fears, her dreams, her frustrations. This allows her to feel heard, to feel competent, acknowledged, and important.

Scripture would suggest that God agrees with this parenting style. In Psalm 66:19–20, David writes, "But God has surely listened and has heard my prayer. Praise be to God, who has not rejected my prayer or withheld his love from me!"

Though He is Lord of the universe, your Father welcomes you to approach His throne any time of any day. He has promised to hear your prayers, whether they be desperate cries for help or songs of thanksgiving. He wants to hear about your every day: your fears, your dreams, your frustrations.

No Time-Outs

Some modern parents are surprised to hear that trauma counselors advise against "time-outs" for children from difficult places. Though clearly a non-violent option for discipline, this punishment runs the risk of driving children away from their parents. In situations where little to no attachment exists, this can be detrimental to the long-term goals for the children.

Authorities suggest pulling the child near instead and asking him to think about his actions.

It is no accident that God, our relationship-driven Abba Father, never casts us from His presence. Hebrews 10:22 advises us, "Let us draw near to God with a sincere heart and with the full assurance that faith brings, having our hearts sprinkled to cleanse us from a guilty conscience and having our bodies washed with pure water."

It is by drawing near to God that we may be cleansed from our guilty conscience.

> *God, our relationship-driven Abba Father, never casts us from His presence.*

Use of Name

Not long ago, a close friend of mine spoke at his grandfather's funeral. Recalling favorite memories of a man who had influenced him greatly, he explained how his grandfather would greet him and his siblings when they were young.

Grandpa would spot his beloveds, bend his knees slightly to approximate their height, clap once, and call them by name. It was a simple gesture, but it made the kids feel noticed and loved.

We all like to be called by name, don't we? Especially by someone prestigious or important. Imagine a movie star or king or Nobel Peace Prize winner passing you on the street and greeting you by name. Wouldn't you feel pretty special? It's also nice to hear your name from someone you love. The first time your child says "Mama" or "Daddy" can set your heart aflutter, as can a voicemail from your true love using your name.

By this point, I'm sure it won't surprise you to learn that authorities in attachment will tell you that it's crucial to use your child's name often. It helps a child feel known and valued.

Do you know that God calls you by your name? John 10:3 tells us, "The gatekeeper opens the gate for him, and the sheep listen to his voice. He calls his own sheep by name and leads them out."

The Almighty calls us by name. Forget movie stars, earthly kings, and Nobel Peace Prize winners. The Star

The Star of David, the King of kings, and the Prince of Peace calls you by name!

of David, the King of kings, and the Prince of Peace calls you by name!

Do-Overs

Attempting to correct a child's misbehavior can be challenging in the best of circumstances. But when the child has a troubled background, it becomes even more complex. Loving parents wrestle with the fine line between communicating clearly that a behavior is not acceptable and disrupting the relationship by conveying frustration or disappointment.

In these circumstances, attachment therapists dependably recommend offering the child a "do-over," an opportunity to replay the situation and respond in a healthier manner. The redo is not intended to be punitive, but instructive. It provides a means of practicing right behavior until it becomes the natural response.[2]

Our merciful Father also gives us redos. Though we may mess up repeatedly, He offers us second chances. And third. And fourth.

Lamentations 3:22–23 says, "Because of the LORD's great love we are not consumed, for his compassions never fail. They are new every morning; great is your faithfulness."

If you're troubled by your own behavior, feeling like you've failed again and again, take heart. Every day, God gives you a fresh new start, a clean slate, *new mercies.* He offers you a do-over!

> *Every day, God gives you a fresh new start, a clean slate,* new mercies.

---

[2] Purvis, et al., *The Connected Child,* 97–98.

Gratitude

During a recent house parent training session in India, we discussed responses to trauma—from sensory processing disorders to hoarding. When we got to the topic of sleeplessness, I offered one simple suggestion: encourage the children who are old enough to start a gratitude journal.

I felt silly instructing this particular group to encourage thankfulness. Just that week—despite imprisonments for their faith and shunning by their families—they had expressed gratitude for God's hand at work in their lives. I knew they modeled this attitude for the children in their care, yet I felt there was something to be said for gratitude specifically as the last thought at night.

Did you know that expressing gratefulness actually prompts your brain to release dopamine, the calm and happy hormone?[3] So when a child thinks of and records a few things for which he can say "thanks," just before closing his eyes at night, it helps him to rest peacefully.

Isn't God amazing? He commands us to "give thanks in all circumstances" (1 Thessalonians 5:18), and when we do, He rewards that obedience in our biological makeup. He gives us a little shot of comfort and rest.

Matching

Another powerful tool in a parent's attachment toolbox is referred to as "matching." This subtle technique of

---

[3] Emily Fletcher, "The Neuroscience of Gratitude," *HuffPost* (blog), November 24, 2015, last modified December 6, 2017, www.huffingtonpost.com/emily-fletcher/the-neuroscience-of-gratitude_b_8631392.html.

mirroring a child—especially his body language—produces a subconscious, but effective, impact. It amplifies a parent's presence by demonstrating synchronicity with the child.

Matching can be as simple as kneeling to a child's level or as deliberate as mimicking her facial expressions. By sitting in the same posture or even copying his noises when he's at play, you can communicate to a child that you are alike. You can begin to talk the same way, gesture similarly, and laugh together the way families do. These hints at bonding can speak volumes to a lonely child's heart.

For children who've known real suffering, matching may be uncomfortable at first. Karyn Purvis, David Cross, and Wendy Lyons Sunshine, trailblazers in their field of attachment and whose primary work was with internationally adopted children, put it this way in their masterwork, *The Connected Child*:

> If you purposely choose the same flavor snack that your little boy has chosen, and then he notices your choice and decides to switch his own to something different, you could be dealing with a traumatized child who feels a strong need for self-protective boundaries. Be patient and respect his comfort level and need for safety and distance.[4]

Being sensitive to the child's uneasiness with bonding allows him to approach the relationship on his terms and timeline. Yet we are assured that, over time, the child

---

[4] Purvis, et al., *The Connected Child*.

will begin to mirror the adult: "As children become more attuned to their families, they will match a parent's stance, voice, and gestures. So remember that your behavior is a model for your child."[5]

Many parents endure years of fiery defiance when a child first joins their family. For the moms and dads who've endured outbursts and protective barriers long enough to—at last—reach the child's first choice to mirror their actions, a victory dance is in order! It is a tremendous compliment and accomplishment when a child determines he wants to be "just like" Mom or Dad.

God shares this joy.

God took on the form of a man so He could amplify His presence in our lives.

Talk about matching! God took on the form of a man so He could amplify His presence in our lives. That's why He came to earth. He matched our behavior, acted like one of us, so that we could attach to Him.

Walter C. Kaiser Jr., President Emeritus of Gordon-Conwell Theological Seminary, shed new light for me on this topic of God made flesh in his article "Israel's Missionary Call" in the *Perspectives on the World Christian Movement: A Reader.*[6] He draws attention to Psalm 67:1–2: "May God be gracious to us and bless us and make his face shine on us—so that your ways may be known on earth, your salvation among all nations." This psalm is actually a restating of a blessing first written in Numbers

---

[5] Ibid.

[6] Walter C. Kaiser Jr., "Israel's Missionary Call," in *Perspectives on the World Christian Movement: A Reader*, 4th ed., eds. Ralph C. Winter and Steven C. Hawthorne (Pasadena, CA: William Carey Library, 2009).

6:24–26. But when David quotes the passage, he makes some small, but impactful changes.

First, he changed the word for "Lord," (the name used in Israel's covenant relationship) to the word "God," (the name used for God as He relates to all men). This is significant because it demonstrates a new, broader family of God. Then he changed the words "upon us" to "among us." The one who came for all men shone His face among us! He became one of us, matching our form, our behavior, our temptations, and our joys. Why? So that "Your ways may be known among the earth, your salvation among the nations." The best way for God's ways to be made known was for Him to mirror our fragile human state.

God Incarnate

We always marvel at Christmastime that God sent His Son to earth as a tiny babe, but really, it's worth our marvel every single day.

It wasn't enough that He took on the form—and limitations—of a man. I mean, couldn't He have just appeared somewhere, full-grown, and started His ministry by calling His disciples? That would have certainly been a tremendous step down for the One who created the universe. But God saw fit to reduce Himself to a fragile and defenseless infant.

He allowed Himself to be dependent upon mere humans.

As an infant, when He waited for Mary to feed Him, do you think He remembered His ability to speak light into being? As He was learning to walk on wobbly toddler legs, do you suppose He wanted to tell His parents He was the One who had parted the Red Sea for their ancestors?

As He learned to speak Hebrew, was He reflecting on the Tower of Babble He'd brought down?

The Mighty One became a baby for us.

It may not be in attachment therapist terms, but Hebrews 4:15 words it like this: "For we do not have a high priest who is unable to empathize with our weaknesses, but we have one who has been tempted in every way, just as we are—yet He did not sin."

Jesus took on flesh to establish a new level of intimacy with His children. He has walked in skin. He knows our fears, our challenges, our joys, and our sorrows.

He also modeled holiness in the hopes that we, His children, would take on His behaviors. He anticipates that we'll one day decide we want to be "just like Dad."

Questions to Ponder or Discuss

Before reading chapter six, read Isaiah 48:17. How have you seen God "direct you in the way you should go?"

After reading the chapter:

1) Have you ever acted out as a means of getting attention? What did you do?

2) Do you think it's important for a child to learn to obey authority? Why or why not?

3) How could you weave more gratitude into your daily life?

CHAPTER 7

Choice

HOW GOD MADE YOU HIS OWN

You're probably familiar with Matthew 22:15–22, but I'll be surprised if you've heard it in the context of orphan ministry before. It begins with some antagonists pretty much jibing Jesus.

You've heard of the Pharisees and the Herodians? Well, normally they weren't pals. The Herodians were loyal to King Herod, while the Pharisees wanted King David's lineage to be restored to the throne. But when it came to Jesus, the two parties agreed: He had to go. He was gaining too many followers through His teachings and miracles. He was upsetting the established order of society and speaking with too much authority. So the Pharisees and the Herodians joined forces, intending to cause Jesus some public humiliation:

> Then the Pharisees went out and laid plans to trap him in his words. They sent their disciples to him

along with the Herodians. "Teacher," they said, "we know that you are a man of integrity and that you teach the way of God in accordance with the truth. You aren't swayed by others, because you pay no attention to who they are. Tell us then, what is your opinion? Is it right to pay the imperial tax to Caesar or not?"

But Jesus, knowing their evil intent, said, "You hypocrites, why are you trying to trap me? Show me the coin used for paying the tax." They brought him a denarius, and he asked them, "Whose image is this? And whose inscription?"

"Caesar's," they replied.

Then he said to them, "So give back to Caesar what is Caesar's, and to God what is God's."

When they heard this, they were amazed. So they left him and went away.

I think it's interesting to note that the Pharisees "sent their disciples." When confronting the Lord of the universe, it's probably wise to send your underlings. But for some reason, I don't think that tactic fooled Jesus.

Anyway, that's not the actual point I'm trying to make here.

The sparring parties join forces and plan a sneak attack. They spring a question on Jesus—in public—about paying the Imperial tax (a tax paid by Roman subjects, not the Romans themselves). They assume His answer will alienate one party or the other. Certainly, that will diminish His following. He can't possibly make both sides happy . . .

You know how it goes. Jesus, in His infinite wisdom, stumps them both by saying that since Caesar's image and inscription are on the coin, they belong to him. He's basically saying that they're simply returning to Caesar what clearly belongs to him. Seems reasonable enough. The plotters scratch their heads and walk away, "amazed."

I've heard many pastors speak on this passage, answering the question of submission to governing authorities and paying taxes. And I agree the common application is valid. Jesus says, "Give back to Caesar what is Caesar's."

One day, when reading this passage, however, I wondered about a new question. Jesus finishes that statement with, "and to God what is God's." We discuss what belongs to Caesar, but isn't it more important to know what belongs to God?

So what is it that is God's that we should be giving back to Him?

Well, let's look at this passage again. How did Jesus say we can know the coin belongs to Caesar? It bears His image and inscription. If that's the litmus test, then anything in God's image or bearing His inscription belongs to Him.

And what, exactly bears God's image and inscription? Genesis 1:27 tells us: "So God created mankind in his own image, in the image of God he created them."

So all of mankind bears God's image. That's you! And me. And my daughter's professor and my son's soccer coach. It's the flight attendant, the nurse, the stock broker, and the garbage man. It's everyone I may encounter on a given day and everyone I don't.

But wait, there's more! What about the inscription? Second Corinthians 3:3 says, "You show that you are a letter from Christ, the result of our ministry, written not with ink but with the Spirit of the living God, not on tablets of stone but on tablets of human hearts."

That letter was written to the church. So "you" means YOU, if you follow Christ and rely on Him for your salvation.

Similarly, 2 Corinthians 1:21–22 says, "Now it is God who makes both us and you stand firm in Christ. He anointed us, set his seal of ownership on us, and put his Spirit in our hearts as a deposit, guaranteeing what is to come."

This means we are not only created in God's image, but if we claim Christ, we also bear His inscription on our hearts.

Do you see the beauty in this? If we bear God's image, it follows that we originally belonged to Him. Just as Caesar had a coin created with his own image and inscription for use in his kingdom and it was to go back to him, God created us and put His own stamp, His image and inscription, upon us for use in His kingdom. And He wants us back!

Revel in that for a moment.

Though we humans become obsessed with money, asking whether we really must pay taxes or tithes or tips, God is obsessed with us! He made us in His image so that there would be no doubt about to whom we belonged. In our every chromosome, God declares His ownership!

In our every chromosome, God declares His ownership!

And in this particular passage, Jesus basically asserts that Caesar can have the money. God wants mankind.

In fact, I believe that God wants us for more than a collection, more than a community. He wants a clan! What he wants is a family—sons and daughters to do life with. His greatest passion is to bring His children back unto Himself to be in relationship with Him.

> *God's greatest passion is to bring His children back unto Himself to be in relationship with Him.*

When we really let this truth resonate through our brains and settle in our hearts, it can be too much to process, let alone comprehend. Why on earth would God want me?

You see, I don't often recognize His image in me. Yet He says I bear it, as do you.

So I guess that begs the question, "What does it mean to be in someone's image?"

In His Image

When our firstborn, Berea, was born, we studied her. We could tell immediately that her almond-shaped eyes, her thick, dark brown hair, her bow-tie lips, and her good set of lungs were all in her daddy's image. I could claim only her long fingers. But she was ours, there was no mistaking that. From birth, she bore our image.

When Noah came along, he appeared to be more of a mix of the two of us. Though he was our second child, we still noted every detail with utter fascination. His face shape was his father's, but his coloring was mine. Clearly, he had gotten his height (described at the time as "length") from his daddy!

If we couldn't attribute a particular feature, we would assume it was because Jim was adopted. We would conclude that his mysterious heritage had superimposed its image onto our child.

In the interest of full disclosure, I must admit what only a parent could understand: To this day, I still find myself pausing to gaze at my children. I marvel at the curl in her hair and the beard on his chin. I know their expressions in ways others would miss. I could identify my child from just a glance at his or her elbow.

I know them. I study them. They are beautiful and bewildering and mine.

Is it possible God studies us, who are made in His image, with the same crazy fascination? Scripture says yes! He knows the very number of hairs on our head (Matthew 10:30).

That's some pretty crazy attention He pays! Imagine. It's not just a matter of remembering—"April, 126,432 hairs." It's a matter of constant monitoring. After a shower, as I'm pulling a clump of hair from the drain, I often wonder, *Did you catch that, God? Minus 567 just now.*

I know He doesn't need my reminding. Or help with math. He's so attentive! He's always gazing on His children, those made in His image.

So why the need to "give back" to God what is God's? He's made it clear we belong to Him.

Here's the problem: We all . . . at some point . . . have chosen not to bear God's image. Like the prodigal son, we have chosen not to live in our Father's house or abide by His rules. We've made bad choices and gone our own ways. We've done things that don't resemble Him at all. We've chosen not to live as children of God, but as orphans.

Of course, it's not what God wants for us. He wants us to live in relationship with Him, staying in His presence and enjoying His provisions. Yet our lust for something outside His kingdom lures us away, promising independence and excitement and pleasure. And we follow with thirsty desire.

And so, God pursues us. It is not enough for Him that He created us and that we bear His image. Despite our wanderings, God's greatest passion is to bring His children back to Himself, into family.

> *Despite our wanderings, God's greatest passion is to bring His children back to Himself, into family.*

What does that look like . . . this bringing children into His family?

The Great Adoption

I think it looks a lot like it does when we bring a child into our family, like adoption.

When I was little, I was surrounded by adoption. My closest friends had been adopted, and I was jealous! These kids had been chosen, but my parents just got stuck with whatever came out.

I always imagined the scene in the hospital room as a letdown for my parents. I was certain their dreams of Gerber-baby smooth cheeks and bright eyes were shattered when the nurse presented wrinkly me. I hadn't been selected for the Walker family team. I landed there by default.

But God—through Scripture—tells me that He chose to adopt me. He wanted me to be His child. And He wants you, too. To convince us, He gives us powerful imagery of orphans and adoption throughout His Word.

God—through Scripture—tells me that He chose to adopt me.

In Ephesians 1:5, the apostle Paul writes that, "he [God] predestined us for adoption to sonship through Jesus Christ, in accordance with his pleasure and will."

What a blessing to know that it is God's *pleasure* to adopt me! Learning this truth comforted me. Perhaps I wasn't chosen by my parents, but I *had* been chosen by God!

This comfort deepened when I was thirteen. I'd like to take you with me on a flashback to one specific day.

The scene was a courtroom. My mom, dad, sister, and I were there, along with a boy named Vincent. We stood together, facing a judge.

Here's the sum of what we knew about Vincent: He was nine years old. He had been shuffled from foster home to foster home for several years and knew the realities that often came with that. A family had adopted his three biological sisters but not him. His current foster home had offered him a steady diet of frozen pizza and *The Dukes of Hazard*.

The judge turned to my parents and in a stern tone asked, "Do you understand the implications of what you are asking me to do today? You will be legally responsible for him. If he gets into any trouble, you will be responsible to make restitution. You will be bound to provide his needs. And he will be granted the same rights and privileges as your two daughters."

My parents looked this young, defenseless boy in the face and said "yes."

And with that yes, they had chosen a son—a boy who would carry their name and live in their home. A young one who would share holidays and report cards and soccer games. A son who would—like all sons—sometimes fail them. But also a son who would be in relationship with them and receive their love and devotion from that moment on.

What an amazing illustration of God's love for us!

Psalm 68:6 tells us that "God sets the lonely in families." It's who He is and what He does. He chooses us as His children and places us in His family.

As I understand it, God had it pretty nice in His throne room. Yet He chose to get messy. Involved. He took on a family of orphans. He knew that we would fail Him sometimes. But still He longed for fellowship with those He created in his own image, even though we had turned from Him.

His courtroom was the cross. Calvary was where God answered the questions that have been reverberating throughout human history . . .

"Will you be legally responsible for this child?"

God answered in Romans 6:23: "For the wages of sin is death, but the gift of God is eternal life in Christ Jesus our Lord." Though this child is bound by sin and owes a debt he can't begin to pay, I choose him. I will be legally responsible and pay the debt he owes.

"Will you provide for her needs?"

God replied through Paul in Philippians 4:19: "And my God will meet all your needs according to the riches of his glory in Christ Jesus." Though she brings nothing to this family, I will provide her every need. Even when she turns to other sources, looking for all she needs, I will not cut her off.

"Ahh. But will you give him all the same rights as your Son, Jesus?"

Galatians. 4:4–7 records God's response:

But when the set time had fully come, God sent his Son, born of a woman, born under the law, to redeem those under the law, that we might receive adoption to sonship. Because you are his sons, God sent the Spirit of his Son into our hearts, the Spirit who calls out, *"Abba,* Father." So you are no longer a slave, but God's child; and since you are his child, God has made you also an heir.

In essence, God promises we who are His children will have the same rights and privileges as His Son, Jesus. His entire kingdom will be shared with us.

We will no longer be lonely. We will be His.

THIS is why John wrote: "See what great love the Father has lavished on us, that we should be called children of God! And that is what we are!" (I John 3:1).

We have been spiritually, legally, and thoroughly adopted by the King of kings and Lord of lords. We have been chosen as His own and called by His name.

He Gotcha!

Within adoption circles, there is a celebratory phenomena called, "Gotcha Day," where families commemorate the day a child was brought into the family, the anniversary of the day the legal adoption was completed. In this media-driven age, many of the families remember by watching a video of the original, momentous day.

Hundreds of these heartwarming Gotcha Day videos are now available online. Many require a box of tissues nearby.

If you have access to YouTube, I'd highly recommend you go watch one of my favorites, "Lucy Lane's Gotcha Day." A simple search will find it.

Seriously. Go to the video and watch for God's love for you!

If you do not know God as your Father, listen for His voice calling today. He has traveled so far from His heavenly throne to bring you into His family. Don't ignore such a great love. Today, you have the opportunity to stop listening to Satan's lies about you, stop trying to pay your debt on your own, stop trying to provide for yourself, stop walking alone, stop forfeiting the rights you have as heir to God's kingdom.

God gives us His word that, as your Father, He'll take care of all of that. In John 1:12, He says, "Yet to all who did receive him, to those who believed in his name, he gave the right to become children of God."

If you DO know God as your Father . . . celebrate Gotcha Day! Watch some videos and relish that Fatherly, pursuing, relentless love God has for you.

But don't stop there. Get wrapped up in God's passion to adopt those whom He has chosen! Look around. See those longing for family and draw them in. Assure them that they, too, have a heavenly Father who loves them.

> *Get wrapped up in God's passion to adopt those whom He has chosen!*

Bear your Father's image in a world that doesn't look much like Him by being passionate about what He's passionate about: the Great Adoption.

Questions to Ponder or Discuss

Before reading chapter seven, read Genesis 1:27. What does it mean that you were made in God's image?

After reading the chapter:

1) What do you typically think of when you hear the words, "in his image?"

2) How has adoption impacted your view of family?

3) Who do you know who's currently not living as one of God's children? How can you show him or her God's love?

4) What does it mean to you that God chose to adopt you?

CHAPTER 8

Comfort

HOW YOU CAN CONSOLE THE HEART OF GOD

It was our last day with a short-term team in Russia's Far East. We decided we'd shadow our baby nurturers, a tenderhearted group we'd hired to go into understaffed, state-run institutions to hold, bathe, and play with the babies living there. They would sing to and play peekaboo with little ones, offering the physical touch and mental stimulation they needed in order to thrive.

We met up with the baby nurturers at a four-room hospital wing that was home to infants who had been abandoned at birth. They remained at the hospital for six to nine months while awaiting paperwork to be completed in order for them to be transferred to a "Dom Rebyonka," or baby orphanage.

The wing was set up with the healthiest babies who were believed to be "typical" down at the farthest end from the nurses' station. These infants had not been left because of their conditions, but because of the parents' circumstances.

The next room contained children who appeared to have some mild issue. Maybe it was webbed fingers or a touch of jaundice.

The third room from the end contained children with more serious challenges. That's where the children with Down syndrome, cleft palates, or fetal alcohol syndrome were placed.

The room closest to the nurses' station housed children with the most serious conditions. I had been told you'd find children with severe deformities, HIV/AIDS, or spina bifida there. Foreigners were not permitted to enter this room.

On this particular day, however, when I entered the abandoned baby wing of the hospital, I could not find any hospital staff—not at the nurses' station, not on the wing. So I decided to go into this room closest to the nurses' station, assuming I could always act as though I hadn't known that I wasn't supposed to be there.

I was nervous, both about how hospital staff would respond to my presence in this forbidden room and about what I would see when I entered.

As I stepped cautiously into the room, I turned to the first bassinet on my right. After shooing the flies away, I picked up a tiny, fresh newborn. He was tightly swaddled, so I could see only his head. It looked perfectly normal, other than a touch of eczema.

I began to rock him in my arms, speaking to him in a high voice I reserve for babies. My eyes met his, and I cooed.

I began to wonder why he had been placed in that

room, since he appeared healthy. I felt the swaddled bundle for appendages and studied his face. I saw no signs of fetal alcohol syndrome or Down syndrome. I could detect no major deformities.

He was so itty bitty that I assumed his mother was still there in the hospital. For one thing, he was clearly a newborn. For another, Russian women typically stay in the hospital much longer than we American women do after giving birth.

So as I held him, I uttered a prayer for his mother. I couldn't imagine the circumstances which led her to give up her son after carrying him for nine months in her womb. Was it too much to hope for a change of heart or situation?

I returned to the bassinet to look for the little guy's name and birth date. I noted that he had not yet been named. This seemed to confirm my assumption that he was perhaps less than even twenty-four hours old. Then I looked at the birth date, and I knew something was very wrong.

According to the birth date, he was actually five months old.

Maybe I wasn't reading the card correctly. Like much of the world, Russians write dates differently than we do in the United States. They write the day and then the month and then the year. So I kept looking at the date and thinking that I must be confused.

I was still stupefied about this little one's age when a nurse stepped into the room. To my surprise, she did not appear angry or kick me out. Frankly, she appeared too busy to be bothered with me. She picked up another baby and began to weigh her. I pointed to the card above the empty bassinet and asked, "Am I reading that card correctly? Was he really born in October?"

"Yes," she said, with a look of pity. "He was born with a heart defect. It's something that would have been surgically corrected right at birth, had he been born in your country. But this is Russia, and he's an orphan."

"We've been feeding him through an IV," she continued, "but his veins keep collapsing. We're on the very last vein we can use now, in his skull. When that one collapses . . ." She didn't complete the sentence, but shook her head, placed the baby she'd weighed back in her bassinet, grabbed a folder, and left the room.

I stood, stunned, looking intently at the baby in my arms. These were his last days.

I began to mourn the fact that this child would die having never looked into his mother's eyes. He would likely breathe his last all alone, in a hospital bassinet. I was certain he'd never been outside to see the sun or feel a breeze. He knew only the routine of IV pricks and collection of data on his vitals.

As I held him tighter now, I assured Him that everything was going to be okay. He would be with Jesus soon. Jesus knew his name and was awaiting him. I prayed. I cried. I rocked and bounced.

Typically, when I serve alongside our baby nurturers, I hold a baby for a bit, then return him to his crib and pick up the next, assuring each child gets a turn at some attention. But not this day. I could not pry this tiny one from my arms.

I hadn't realized how much time had passed until a teammate poked his head into the room to ask, "Aren't we supposed to be going now?" I looked at my watch and realized we had overstayed our time slot permitted by the hospital.

Regrettably, I returned the unnamed little one to his bassinet, to a painful and lonely fate.

We gathered our things and left the hospital.

We returned to the hotel and spent the evening packing up our belongings. In the wee hours of the morning, we caught a plane headed for home.

Not at Home in Indiana

Home didn't feel like home for me. I was where I belonged. I had my family around me, I was surrounded by folks speaking my mother tongue, and I could sleep in my own bed. Yet my heart wasn't there. It was with a baby who knew no home, an infant who may not even be alive anymore.

I tried to homeschool my kids, to meal plan, to catch up on rest. I blamed jetlag and fatigue, but there was something more stopping me from re-entering my own world. I could not shake thoughts of this baby I had held to my heart.

I began to get angry as I interfaced with my own culture. Those around me discussed football championships, skin care, and home improvements. I couldn't even enter into the conversations because none of it mattered to me. My mind was preoccupied with very different questions: Was the baby I held still alive? Was anyone with him right now? Could I get back to him in time? If I did, would I be permitted even to see him?

This inability to function as normal began to worry me. Would I ever return to myself? Could I focus on my own responsibilities again?

My only consolation was the knowledge that our baby nurturers visited his hospital wing. Hopefully he was being held for some small portion of each long day.

At last, I began flipping through my journal, looking for reminders of God's faithfulness to me, for signs of hope or inspiration. I landed on an entry I wrote not long before the trip on which I met the nameless baby.

"Lord," I had written, "would You help me feel You? Would you allow me not just to know about You in my head, but to also know You intimately in my heart?"

You see, I'm a pretty logical person. Whenever I take one of those personality inventories and there's a scale from feeling to thinking, I land way over on the thinking side. I enjoy studying and learning but often fear I appear unfeeling, especially among women.

I've often sat in a Bible study, absorbed in the connotations of some word in the Greek when I look up to discover that all the other women in the circle are crying. Caught off guard, I realize I'm completely missing something.

I had begun to envy those women. I was jealous that they could be moved with such compassion or sorrow or beauty. I had grown resentful of women who could walk in the door with "the joy of the Lord" glowing off of them. I wanted a piece of that emotional connection to the Lord and others, but it felt out of reach for me.

When I read that journal entry again, just a month or so later, I knew that God—in His faithfulness—had answered my request. I realized that this pain I was feeling was shared.

Oh, it's not what I had in mind when I asked Him to let me feel with Him. No. I was expecting warm fuzzies and feel-good vibes. But what I had was the real thing . . . real emotion, real perspective, real God. Because I knew that when God sees that baby lying—alone—in a hospital bassinet, it breaks His heart even more than it broke mine. He loves that child, and that baby never leaves His mind.

What's more, I realized that He is continually aware—not only of that boy in the bassinet, but every baby in that room next to the nurses' station. He knows their stories, their conditions, the number of hairs on their sweet and tiny heads.

Actually, He is bigger still. He knows all of the babies in that hospital . . . all of the babies in that city in Russia's cold Far East. He is intimately acquainted with the little ones in Russia and around the globe, and it is a tremendous burden to bear.

At my request, He had given me just a glimpse.

A New Paradigm

This realization gave me new insight into the biblical story found in Matthew 25 about the sheep and the goats. Jesus says to those to whom He is about to grant entrance into His kingdom,

> "'Come, you who are blessed by my Father; take your inheritance, the kingdom prepared for you since the creation of the world. For I was hungry

and you gave me something to eat, I was thirsty and you gave me something to drink, I was a stranger and you invited me in, I needed clothes and you clothed me, I was sick and you looked after me, I was in prison and you came to visit me. . . .' Whatever you did for one of the least of these brothers and sisters of mine, you did for me." (vv. 34–36, 40)

Just as the knowledge that our baby nurturers visited that hospital in Russia's Far East brought comfort to my aching heart, we can bring comfort to God's heart by caring for "the least of these." We can alleviate a bit of the sorrow and grief He bears as He sees His children in pain and need.

It is an overwhelming thought!

Little ole April—with no importance or talent or impressive birthright—can minister to the heart of God.

You—when you hold a child, speak a blessing, or share a meal—can apply salve to the very heart of the Creator God. You can minister to Him by relieving the pain He feels over the condition of His beloved children.

> *You—when you hold a child, speak a blessing, or share a meal—can apply salve to the very heart of the Creator God.*

This reality has changed my motivation for ministry. I no longer minister because I see the needs of orphans, as dire as they are. I minister, knowing that I am bringing relief to the very heart of God.

Questions to Ponder or Discuss

Before reading chapter eight, read Matthew 25:36. How could you demonstrate care for "the least of these?"

After reading the chapter:

1) What do you typically think of when you read Matthew 25:36?

2) Did any portrayal of God in this chapter bother you? If so, what and why?

3) How do you feel when you consider that you could bring comfort to the heart of God?

CHAPTER 9

Confrontation

HOW YOU CAN MODEL GOD'S LOVE BY CONFRONTING THE ORPHAN CRISIS

Each chapter leading to this one has begun with a story—from my own life, an orphan's, or the Bible. But this chapter is one I'd like for *you* to write or continue. It's time to discover your own path, your own response to God's love for you and His call to the orphan.

If you've made it this far through this book, you've read that God's command to care for orphans is clear. You've seen how obeying that call not only offers glimpses of God's character but also helps to develop it in you. You've reflected on your role as a chosen and beloved child of God . . . and seen in new ways how passionately He loves and pursues you.

Hopefully, you've also come to understand that *you* can minister to the very heart of the creator God by caring for orphans. That amazing privilege just cannot be ignored.

And so the question surfaces: What will you do?

Now, please don't close this book, assuming I'm going to tell you that you're obligated to sell everything you own, move overseas, and feed hungry children. God may tell you that, but I won't. It's not my place.

And don't jump to the conclusion that I think every Christian is obligated to adopt. I do not. I have not.

In fact, you may have heard it proposed in church circles that if only 7 percent of the world's Christians were to adopt, there would be no orphan crisis. But I'll argue that assertion with two points. The first is that—according to Scripture—we are all called to care for orphans. Even if 7 percent of the world's Christians *were* to adopt, that wouldn't allow the other 93 percent of us to sit and do nothing.

An even bigger problem with that plan for solving the orphan crisis is that only 1 percent of the world's orphans are available for adoption.[1] One percent!

Why? Because many of the nations with the largest populations of orphans are places where mothers are typically not ushered into sterile environments and offered epidurals when the time comes to give birth. They are not assisted by a caseworker with filing official documentation, giving the newborn a legal identity.

Without a paper trail—in the absence of legal identity—no adoption can be processed.

So 99 percent of the world's orphans have no hope of a forever family.

Of course, I hope it's clear by now that I am a fan of adoption. If that's what God's calling you to do, I

---

[1] Diane Elliot, *The Global Orphan Crisis: Be the Solution, Change Your World* (Chicago: Moody Publishers, 2012).

will cheer you on. I have celebrated the process with families, held their hands through the challenges, and prayed for them as they model God's redemptive love to a watching world.

Ninety nine percent of the world's orphans have no hope of a forever family.

But I also continue to serve a tiny portion of the 99 percent and do my best to recruit others to join me.

Visit Orphans

Having read chapter two, you won't be surprised that I'll open the list of ways to help orphans by suggesting you visit them. Not only do I recommend this because James 1:27 encourages us to visit them, but also because meeting orphans face-to-face is the best way to understand them, their needs, their potential, and their day-to-day lives. Once you've met some orphans and vulnerable children, you're in a better position to determine your role in helping them, and you're certainly better equipped and more motivated to pray for them!

Sadly, short-term mission trips have gotten a bad rap recently. And, honestly, we don't have to look too far to see why.

Examples of harm done by short-term teams abound. I've read stories of churches in South America being painted twenty times in a five-year span because it was a good way to occupy the visiting Americans. A long-term ministry in Russia was kicked out of a school they had worked long and hard to develop a relationship with when a short-termer took a photo without permission. I've also heard a number of accounts of fake orphanages being set up in Africa when foreigners come. Children from the village gather and stare up at the eyes of their visitors, and somebody pockets donations—lots of them.

Worse, children can actually be taken from their families to create a similar scenario.

But don't rule out the opportunity to serve overseas too quickly! God still uses short-term mission teams.

With healthy policies in place, short-term teams can be a tremendous benefit to long-term ministries. They can offer a fresh boost of energy, complete a much-needed project, or become prayer warriors with a passion and commitment they never would have had without visiting the field.

So how do you know if a team you're considering joining is a good one? Will you make an impact or a mess?

To ensure you're making the best choice possible, ask the following questions before joining a short-term team.

1) What is the long-term plan to support those we'll serve during this short-term ministry experience?

The big picture is important. God calls us to "go, make disciples of all the nations" (Matthew 28:19), so you want to be certain that your short-term trip experience holds the promise of leading to discipleship.

Let me be frank. Disciples are not made in a six-day span.

To think that I could revolutionize the world by taking a short-term trip would be pretty prideful. But I could be used to support an organization that's in it for the long haul, doing the work day in and day out.

For example, one guy picks out a village from a map of Zimbabwe, shows up, and drops off hundreds of pairs of shoes.

Is it nice? Well, as long as the primary employer in that village isn't a shoe company, yes. Does it make disciples? Probably not.

In another example, a guy asks a ministry he respects what he could do that would be helpful. They request shoes for a village in Zimbabwe so that children will be permitted to attend school. So he takes hundreds of pairs of shoes, and they hold an event for the community in their new church. The hospitality the community experiences makes them feel so welcome, they begin coming weekly.

Is it nice? Yes. Does it make disciples? Quite possibly!

Without this long-term vision, many short-term efforts are little different than humanitarian efforts by secular organizations.

Before you select your short-term ministry experience, be certain it is part of a long-term strategy to make disciples.

2) What training will I receive before, during, and after traveling with you?

Many well-intentioned folks jump on a plane with plans to change the world, but if they haven't taken the time to learn about the culture they're entering, there's a huge risk that they'll do more damage than good.

An organization with solid experience in a foreign field will be able to prepare you to be ambassadors for Christ in a new setting. They'll also alert you to any immunizations you should have prior to travel, and help you with fundraising and applying for a visa, if one is needed. What's more, they'll walk you through the experience by continuing the training while you're immersed in the culture and help you process everything for the most long-term benefits after you return home.

3) Does the mission we'll carry out fill a need expressed by those we hope to serve?

Imagine you're at home one day, getting dinner on the table. The doorbell rings, and when you open your front door, there stands a group of fourteen in matching T-shirts. They announce, "We're here to paint your garage!"

Unless you've asked for help with painting your garage . . . or at least acknowledged that your garage needs a fresh coat of paint, life just got really awkward. You'd probably wonder, *Why have they come to my house? Has the neighborhood complained that my garage is in bad repair? Do they think I can't paint?*

In most cases, an international team would have at least sent an email before showing up at the door, but the result is pretty much the same. Gracious hosts around the world allow Americans to have their way, but in the meantime, they can feel stripped of their dignity.

Look for an organization that is sensitive to the felt needs of the people they hope to serve. Otherwise, you risk communicating that those you visit have a way of life that isn't acceptable. That's probably not the best way to establish the kind of relationship that invites meaningful discipleship.

4) How do you promote attachment between orphans and their caregivers while bringing teams in and out of their lives?

One of the greatest challenges those who care for orphans face is forming a healthy attachment with them. Because most of the children enter their care after experiencing neglect, trauma, and abuse, it is quite difficult to build trust.

If the children see their livelihood is supported by the ever-rotating foreign faces at their door, they may not feel the security of knowing that their needs will be met consistently. They often find it difficult to attach to their house parents, as they are constantly on the lookout for the next visitors to impress.

This toxic cycle undermines the efforts of those who work tirelessly, changing wet bed sheets, wiping noses, preparing meals, tutoring geography, and sharing Bible stories.

Showing up for a few days and spoiling the cute kids with trinkets and day trips is fun, and it makes for great photos. But if it isn't handled very carefully, in a manner that actually drives the children toward relationship with their caregivers, it is not in the best interest of the children.

Our goal should always be to make disciples of Christ.

Again, keep the big picture in mind and ask, "How can we help make these children disciples of Christ?" It's going to be by supporting the caregivers who have a long-term impact in the children's lives and meeting their needs.

5) What will we be doing that the host partners can't do for themselves?

Be sure the organization you select is not so bent on creating an experience for Americans that they take work—or dignity—from the community. Sadly, many well-meaning ministries have crippled the communities they hoped to serve by taking employment opportunities from them. This situation not only feeds the cycle of poverty but also creates a culture of dependency and feelings of ineptness.

Ideally, the ministry you join will work in partnership with leaders on the field (the host culture and/or long-term missionaries) to create a mutually beneficial interaction. The nationals will have opportunities to share with or educate the visiting team, and the team will have the opportunity to serve, as well.

For additional considerations before selecting your short-term mission to orphans, visit www.boazproject.org/11questions.

With some thoughtful planning, a mission trip can be the most challenging, rewarding, heartbreaking, or inspiring experience of a lifetime . . . often, all at once! Not only can you have a vital ministry to "the least of these," but you can also encourage missionaries and their partners. You'll likely learn a lot—from words in a foreign language to a new level of dependence upon the Lord.

So don't pass up the opportunity to obey God's commands to visit orphans, to care for widows, to serve the poor. Just be sure the team you join is well-planned, and go confidently, ready to watch God at work!

Of course, not everyone is in a position or stage of life where taking an international trip is an option. Don't worry; I've still got some meaningful alternatives for you. Keep reading!

Additional Practical Steps

The list of possible ways to serve orphans and vulnerable children is nearly endless. My hope for the remainder of this chapter is to give you a wide enough sampling of ideas that you realize that at any stage of life, with any gifting, any income level, or any educational background, there is something you can do. So read on! Note the options listed that interest you. Brainstorm additional ideas. Then pray and determine which God is nudging you to do.

To get started, you'll likely need to vet some orphan care organizations to determine where you'd like to "plug in." While it's convenient to support one in your geographic locale, I'd propose that it's even more important to choose one whose values and methodologies are similar to your own. These days, the internet allows us to be connected in ways that facilitate involvement across great distances, so don't let miles deter you.

> *While it's convenient to support one in your geographic locale, I'd propose that it's even more important to choose one whose values and methodologies are similar to your own.*

Rather, I'd consider the following criteria when choosing an organization to support:

1) How does the organization empower caregivers to attach to the children in their care?

As we discussed in chapter five, research will tell you that the number one determinate for a child overcoming trauma is an attachment to a safe, nurturing adult.

Caregivers may rotate according to a schedule or come into life after so much trauma and independence that attachment is nearly impossible to achieve. Or there may be so many siblings or such intense hunger that parents are present, just not available to tend to a child.

It is in this scenario—when a child is not thoroughly attached to any adult—that intervention from foreigners can disrupt any attempts at relationships with adults who are geographically present. Suddenly, this organization or individual, like a knight in shining armor from across the ocean, may be perceived as salvation! A child becomes convinced, "They will meet my needs. They will feed me. They will send me to school. My parent/caregiver/community cannot. They are impotent, but these foreigners will provide."

In this situation, even the most devoted caregiver who changes wet sheets in the night, wipes noses, helps with homework, and tucks into bed will be rendered unable to form the full attachment that assures the child, "I've got you. You are free to be a child because I will take care of you."

It is crucial that aid is handled in a way that supports a child's attachment to his caregiver and doesn't detract from it.

2) Does the organization's strategy single out specific children?

If help is not offered to each child in a family or community, rivalry—if not outright hazing—can ensue. For this reason, it is important that organizations that funnel donations to assist children be community-focused, never creating divisions within families or institutions.

In a similar vein, a child should never be refused the rights, privileges, or assistance other children in his community receive based on gender, race, religion, or any other factor.

3) Is the organization cautious regarding their overhead expenses?

I'm the first to admit that it takes overhead to run a non-profit effectively. From staff salaries to spreading the word about the good work they do, there are costs involved in charitable causes. I'm always grateful to the donors who recognize this and contribute toward it because—let's face it—orphans can't pay for the services they need!

Of course, administrative costs must have their limits, too.

There's a lot of debate over what percentage of an organization's income "should" go to overhead. I'm not here to prescribe an answer, but I do think you should know where your money is going and be comfortable with it.

Don't be afraid to ask hard questions about where your donations would go. Nonprofits should be prepared and willing to answer.

4) Does the organization respect the role of local community leaders?

Imagine the scene described in Matthew 8, Mark 5, and Luke 8: Jesus and his posse of disciples still have wet feet, they've so recently pulled ashore in Gerasenes. Suddenly, a naked, demon-possessed man appears and begins yelling at Jesus.

Now, this dude was obviously not your typical guy. Despite the locals' attempts to detain him—chaining him hand and foot and assigning guards to watch over him—he manages to escape, tear off his clothes and live in tombs.

Yes, tombs. As in, with dead, smelly bodies.

You know how the story goes. Jesus commands the demons—a legion of them—to leave the man and go instead into some pigs. The pigs turn into a squealy mob and jump off a cliff into the water below and drown.

By the time the amazed onlookers peel their eyes away from the noisy, failed pork venture, the man is sitting at Jesus's feet. Calmly. Dressed. Chill.

Now the rest of the townspeople get freaked out and tell Jesus to leave. So, obligingly, Jesus heads back to the boat. The man He delivered from demon possession begs to go with Him.

Surprisingly, Jesus turns to him and says, "Return home and tell how much God has done for you."

Wait. Go home? Why?

This man had a life-changing experience that clearly made him among the most devoted of devotees. He surely would have followed Jesus anywhere! But the Lord sent him home.

Well, He didn't just send him home. He sent him home *to tell how much God had done for him.*

You see, this guy had a bit of a reputation in Gerasenes. I mean, certainly there had been town hall meetings to discuss potential means of controlling him, shifts for the guards they all pitched in to hire, search parties after escapes.

Only they could know the real transformation that had taken place that day.

Sure, he could cross the lake to Galillee with Jesus and tell folks there. However, they had never smelled him. They hadn't heard his wild screams or seen him running naked. They may be tempted to think this sideshow with Jesus was an act for hire.

But not in Gerasenes. They knew the deal. *They knew this man was one of their own, delivered.*

This is the same reason I believe in partnering with nationals to minister to orphans. Their communities can see that caring for children is not accomplished unto a "foreign god." It is not done according to strange customs or in an unfamiliar language.

Rather, caring for orphans is done in a way that feels comfortable in their culture, by people who speak the same language and crave the same foods as their neighbors. It's carried out by folks who dress the way they do and shop at the same market. It's not done by an outsider who comes with strange solutions or a foreign focus. This selfless, lavish love for orphans is demonstrated by one of their own, delivered.

Roll Up Your Sleeves

Once you've done your research and selected an organization through which you can care for orphans, you'll discover a wide array of ways to get involved. As a springboard, you may want to grab the free, one-page "30 Days of Orphan Care" download from www.boazproject.org/download/8764. There, you'll find thirty quick, actionable steps you can take to begin your orphan care journey. Then, consider jumping on board in one of the following ways:

Volunteer. See if there's a reputable orphan-care ministry near you where you could invest a few hours doing some hands-on work. Those who stuff envelopes for a mailing, handwrite thank you notes, shred documents, or help us pack for Vacation Bible School trips are a huge blessing to us at The Boaz Project!

Leverage your social media platform. Follow your favorite organization on Instagram, Facebook, or Twitter, then "like," share, and comment to help increase our exposure to others who may be looking for ways to help orphans.

Host an event to raise awareness and funds to benefit orphans. It could be an art show, a concert, or a treasure hunt. The options are limited only by your imagination.

Learn. The more you can learn about orphans and the organizations that serve them, the better prepared you'll be to help. As a primer on all things orphan, I recommend *The Global Orphan Crisis: Be the Solution, Change Your*

World by my friend Diane Lynn Elliot. This informative resource covers the causes of the crisis, the factors that make solving it challenging, as well as suggestions for how you can get involved.

Additional resources I'd recommend can be found at www. boazproject.org/knowledgebase/book-list-orphan-care.

Provide an evening of respite for some foster parents you know by offering to babysit or bring dinner.

Create a video for an organization you love, either by traveling on one of their short-term missions trips or using footage they already have on hand.

Gather and recycle metal, then donate the proceeds to your favorite charity serving orphans.

Share your resources by making financial donations to organizations you know and trust. This may be in the form of providing monthly support for an orphanage, taking care of a specific need they have, or even helping a staff member with their expenses.

Register for shopping benefits through some of the retailers offering charitable perks for your business. Check out Amazon Smile, for example. Many grocery stores offer these incentives, as well. This is a simple, no-cost-to-you means of contributing to the financial support needed to provide aid for orphans.

Enable someone to go on a short-term trip, even if the timing isn't good for you. By praying for and financially contributing to another's ministry experience, you can have a tangible outreach to orphans in need. You can also provide a life-changing experience for the missionary and bolster his or her commitment to serving children in need.

Include a deserving organization in your will. Your legacy will include caring for "the least of these."

Have a lemonade stand and donate the proceeds to help orphans.

Host a birthday party for Jesus. Have guests bring a gift that will go to orphans.

Have your child donate his or her spare change to an Orphan Gift Bank, assuring an orphan will have a gift to open on his or her birthday or on Christmas. (Information is available at www.boazproject.org/help/ogb.)

If you're in business, **ask customers to "round up"** their total owed to the nearest dollar, five dollars, or ten dollars, depending upon the price point of your goods or services, explaining that it will help an orphaned child.

Most importantly, pray. Pray for orphans around the world and in your own neighborhood. Pray for organizations serving them, that we would be compassionate, effective, and persuasive in our methods. Pray for caregivers who make moment-by-moment sacrifices to meet the needs of the children in their care, and pray for the church to embrace God's call to serve orphans.

You can sign up for specific requests from The Boaz Project at www.boazproject.org/about.

What about Children in the US?

You may be wondering, *What about the orphans in my own home town?*

Having worked with orphans internationally for nearly twenty years now, I'm often asked, "But what about the kids right here in the US? There are some kids in terrible situations here, too." And I figure for every person who asks, there's likely another three who wonder but don't give their question voice because they don't want to appear confrontational.

So let me begin by saying that I believe that every child conceived bears the image of God. He is worthy of love and opportunity, of protection and nurture. Every human is worthy of dignity and should be given a voice.

For me, the focus of ministry is not about trying to value any one people group over another. It is about serving where God leads me to serve. Along the way, however, I have discovered several valid reasons to concentrate my efforts on children outside the United States. For now, I'll discuss four of them:

> *Every child conceived bears the image of God.*

1) The need . . . according to percentage.

I want to be careful here. Please understand that I am not ranking the extremity of need. I do recognize that children exist in dire, horrific situations here in America. And it grieves my heart.

What I *am* saying is that the numbers of children affected in the US are fewer in comparison. Here's what I mean: According to UNICEF, there are 140 million orphans in our world today.[2] And we have 427,910 children in our foster care system.[3]

Know what that means? The US is home to just 0.3 percent of the world's orphans.

More than 99 percent of the world's orphans live outside of the US!

> *More than 99 percent of the world's orphans live outside of the US!*

While some children suffer unthinkable horrors in our own states (and if you decide to help one, I will root for you!), most of us cannot fathom what it is like in a nation like India, where 9 percent of all children are orphans or Kenya, where 13 percent of all children are orphans.[4]

2) The unlikelihood of adoption.

Though 111,820 children await adoption in the US foster care system, they have a greater hope of a forever family

---

[2] "Orphans," June 16, 2017, UNICEF, accessed January 16, 2018, https://www. unicef.org/media/media_45279.html.

[3] "Statistics (Foster Care Statistics)," Christian Alliance for Orphans, accessed January 16, 2018, https://cafo.org/ovc/statistics/. http://www.orphanoutreach. co/countries-we-serve/india/

[4] "Facts about India," Orphan Outreach, accessed January 16, 2018, http://www. orphanoutreach.co/countries-we-serve/india/; UNICEF, *The State of the World's Children 2012: Children in an Urban World* (New York: UNICEF, 2012).

than the majority of orphans in the world.[5] Why? Because Americans account for nearly half of the adoptions in the entire world, and 78 percent of those are domestic.[6]

With a lower orphan population and a higher number of adoptions, adoptable children in the US have a greater prospect of finding a family to call their own than most around the globe.

3) The enormity of the task.

The orphan crisis is overwhelming. No matter where we begin our efforts, someone will be left out.

So, if you were to find out that friends were adopting, would you ask them "Why adopt that kid and not this one?" I hope not. I hope you'd celebrate the expanding family and do all you can to support and encourage it.

In the same way, we need to applaud every effort to help children who haven't yet been—or will never be—adopted, regardless of their location. The task is great, and it will only be accomplished one child at a time. So instead of fussing over which child, let's get busy helping one.

No individual, organization, or denomination is equipped to adequately care for 140,000,000 orphans. But if each of us does what we're called to, those precious children will know they have a heavenly Father who loves

---

[5] "Statistics (Foster Care Statistics)," Christian Alliance for Orphans.

[6] United Nations Department of Economic and Social Affairs, Population Division, *Child Adoption: Trends and Policies* (New York: United Nations, 2009), 17, http://www.un.org/esa/population/publications/adoption2010/child_adoption.pdf; Jedd Medefind, *Becoming Home: Adoption, Foster Care, and Mentoring—Living Out God's Heart for Orphans* (Grand Rapids, MI: Zondervan, 2013), 21.

them! In the end, the important thing is for each Christ follower to be faithful to do *something* to care for the orphans He loves so dearly.

There's a lot at stake here. Not only do we have a responsibility to care for precious children who are struggling to survive on their own, but we also have an obligation to model the compassion God has extended to each of us.

> *Not only do we have a responsibility to care for precious children who are struggling to survive on their own, but we also have an obligation to model the compassion God has extended to each of us.*

When we selflessly step outside our own needs and those of our immediate family, the world takes note. More than any sermon, our acts of kindness get attention. In a world of divisive rhetoric and hateful speech, the unbelieving are looking for someone to demonstrate Christ's love, to walk in it. I can think of no more powerful means to do that than by caring for orphans.

Let's give them something to talk about!

Questions to Ponder or Discuss

Before reading chapter nine, read Matthew 28:19. What does that command have to do with orphan care?

After reading the chapter:

1) How do you feel about short-term mission trips?

2) Can you think of additional criteria not listed in this chapter which should be considered before taking a short-term mission trip?

3) Have you ever served orphans or considered serving them? In what capacity?

CHAPTER 10

Conclusion

HOW TO EMBRACE YOUR ROLE AS GOD'S CHILD

Imagine trying to explain to a group of orphans that God is their heavenly Father. Father? What's that?

Many orphans have no recollection of a father. So, at best, he's a distant notion. A vacancy. A mystery tinged with sorrow.

Others do remember their fathers, and for most of *them*, the connotation is even more negative. He was likely abusive, neglectful, angry.

So why in the world would they want anything to do with a God who describes Himself as their Father? A heavenly Father? He is even more formidable, with the power to completely destroy.

> *Many orphans have no recollection of a father. So, at best, he's a distant notion. A vacancy. A mystery tinged with sorrow.*

Faced with this dilemma, I asked a group of orphans in Russia to describe the *ideal* father. "What would he be like, this father, if he were absolutely perfect?"

Their answers were enlightening. They didn't mention that he'd play catch with them in the yard or coach their soccer team or let them drive his car. No, in their bravest dreams, they imagined something much simpler.

"He would live in an apartment and let me live there, too," one said.

"He would give me food," chimed in another.

"Good!" I encouraged the feedback. "Anything else?"

They looked at each other blankly. What more could they want?

Seconds ticked by.

At last, with some prodding and a bit of leading, they agreed that the perfect dad would not hurt a mom and would maybe even defend the family if it were being attacked by a violent robber.

I was in a tough spot. To raise their expectations of God was to further disappoint them in their earthly fathers. But I wanted desperately for them to know how richly they are loved.

"Imagine a dad who has not just an apartment, but a mansion!" I said. "And He not only lets you live there but wants you to share the very best room with Him, because He always wants you nearby. He just loves having you close!

"He's a great chef and feeds you just what you need every day. Sometimes it's the most amazing stuff you've ever tasted. Sometimes you don't like it so much. But it's what's best for you, so He helps you get it down. He wants you to grow and be healthy.

"He gives you good advice and helps you with your problems," I added.

"Now imagine He shares everything He has with you . . . His car, His family, His time. THAT is the Father the Bible talks about, and your heavenly Father is not pretend. He's real, and you are His child."

> *Your heavenly Father is not pretend. He's real, and you are His child.*

The Gift of Sonship

Friend, I don't know what kind of earthly father you had, whether he was strict and harsh, present and loving, or altogether absent. I don't know if he assured you of your worth or complained about your very existence.

Yet there is one thing I do know about your earthly father: he pales in comparison to your heavenly one.

After spending these chapters together, I cannot leave you without stating this simple fact: you are loved.

> *You are loved.*

Psalm 139:1–6 assures you that God knows you thoroughly. It says:

You have searched me, LORD, and you know me. You know when I sit and when I rise; you perceive my thoughts from afar. You discern my going out and my lying down; you are familiar with all my ways. Before a word is on my tongue you, LORD, know it completely. You hem me in behind and before, and you lay your hand upon me. Such knowledge is too wonderful for me, too lofty for me to attain.

No earthly father can compare! This love God has for you is so attentive, so intimate, so complete.

Just as the Russian orphans with whom I discussed the ideal father could not fathom a good dad, you cannot comprehend the depth of love our heavenly Father has for you.

Of course, whether you've had a father (or a mother) present in your life or not, you may at times feel like an orphan. You may feel unloved, unwanted, or unnoticed. But look at what God says about that in Isaiah 49:15: "Can a mother forget the baby at her breast and have no compassion on the child she has borne? Though she may forget, I will not forget you!"

As unnatural and uncomfortable as the thought of a mother neglecting her own child may be, we live in a world where such tragic things take place. Parents abandon their own. Or sometimes they reside at the same address, but the home still feels vacant. Sometimes, the best parents cannot fill the ache we have to be known and loved.

Yet God promises never to forget you. He is always with you, hearing your cries and meeting your needs. If that sometimes still doesn't feel like enough, I have a word of hope for you: Your heavenly Father does more than perform the perfunctory duties we often associate with fatherhood. Oh, He's a good provider. He disciplines when necessary. He defends His own. He is available anytime we may have need of Him, and He longs for us to come into His presence.

But do you know what I find most fascinating, most endearing?

Zephaniah 3:17 tells us that our God is *One who dotes*. Catch this: "The LORD your God is with you, the Mighty Warrior who saves. He will take great delight in you; in His love he will no longer rebuke you, but will rejoice over you with singing."

Isn't it an amazing thing to ponder? The Lord of the universe sees you. He knows you. He calls you by name, and He calls you His own. He meets your needs before you speak them. And on top of all of that, He takes delight in you and sings over you!

I pray this truth is embedded in your heart in a new way after reading this book, and that His abundant love changes your every day from here on out.

Always remember: Your heavenly Father is crazy about you!

Activity: After reading the conclusion, try writing a letter to God, telling Him how you feel about being His chosen child.

Acknowledgments

This book would not be possible without the influence of many who've encouraged, mentored, and shared their stories with me. The following list of names will not be exhaustive, but is my attempt to give just a bit of honor where it is due.

To my alma mater, Taylor University, thank you for taking seriously your mission "to develop servant leaders marked with a passion to minister Christ's redemptive love and truth to a world in need." Your influence enabled me to hear God's call to ministry and equipped me to face the challenges along the way. Your partnership over the years has blessed The Boaz Project with a steady flow of qualified short-term teams, interns, donors, and even employees. I'm thrilled that you now enable students to major in orphans and vulnerable children and prepare them to tackle the global orphan crisis in an informed and compassionate manner. Despite the many years since my graduation, you continue to inspire and motivate me.

Thanks are certainly due to my husband, Jim. Without your steadfast belief in me, I never would have seen this book to completion.

My editor, Ashley Casteel, deserves thanks for polishing this manuscript and for mastering formatting and punctuation rules. Your flexibility and patience with my travel schedule and new author mistakes were invaluable in the writing process. You've gone above and beyond the role of editor to become a cheerleader just when I needed it.

I must express my gratitude to Diane Elliot. I'm grateful to you not only for writing the foreword to this book but also for being openhanded with your contacts, time, and enthusiasm.

I also must give shout outs to Courtney Kraus for reading the very first draft of this work and offering constructive feedback, to Jared Davenport for producing the video trailer, and to Noah Jurgensen for constructing www.apriljurgensen.com.

The house parents I'm privileged to know through my work with The Boaz Project are truly my heroes. They not only take on routine parenting tasks (wiping noses, helping with homework, tucking into bed, and changing wet sheets) for multiple children but also accept the difficulties associated with children from hard places (hoarding, lying, nightmares, etc.). Thank you for doing all of it "as unto the Lord," and for giving me permission to enter your homes and lives so freely.

I also must acknowledge the orphans who've taught me so much over the years. Most will never know the influence they've had on me as they modeled resilience, kindness, faith, and humility. You are so loved!

And of course, I owe the greatest debt to my heavenly Father for adopting me as His own.

You've read the book. Now join the experience!

Model God's all-encompassing Fatherly love by caring for orphans. Visit www.boazproject.org/trips today and choose the right schedule and destination for *you* to visit orphans.

This is your opportunity to:

- See God's face in the children you serve
- Minister to the heart of God
- Watch for miracles
- Demonstrate "faultless religion"
- Share Christ's love
- Join a community of folks committed to loving orphans and their caregivers

The Boaz Project will be with you every step of the way.

If you enjoyed *The Orphan's Abba*, please leave a review on Amazon, letting others know why. Then, connect with the author at www.AprilJurgensen.com and The Boaz Project at www.boazproject.org

About the Author

Fueled by a relentless passion for children and justice, April Jurgensen is the founder and executive director of The Boaz Project, Inc., a nonprofit organization that inspires and equips leaders around the globe to care for orphans in their own communities. For two decades she has impacted vulnerable children by addressing their physical, spiritual, and educational needs.

Between trips to visit the children who've stolen her heart, April seizes opportunities to write and speak about them. She brings the experience and insight from more than one hundred international trips to her messages.

April holds a BA in writing from Taylor University in Upland, Indiana. In addition to loving her occupation, she is crazy about her husband, Jim, and their two adult children, Berea and Noah. When they aren't globetrotting, the Jurgensens call Greenwood, Indiana, home.

Made in the USA
Columbia, SC
02 November 2018